WITHDRAWN

INSTITUTE OF INTERNATIONAL STUDIES
YALE UNIVERSITY

The Mediterranean

ITS ROLE IN AMERICA'S FOREIGN POLICY

The Yale Institute of International Studies was organized in 1935 for the purpose of promoting research and training in the field of international relations. Although concerned with all aspects of international affairs, its studies have been primarily devoted to clarifying contemporary problems in the foreign policy of the United States. The present publication, "The Mediterranean: Its Role in America's Foreign Policy," analyses the nature of the American interest in terms of the essential features of the region.

Earlier publications of the Institute are: A. Whitney Griswold's "Far Eastern Policy of the United States," George T. Davis' "A Navy Second to None," Arnold Wolfers' "Britain and France between Two Wars," Nicholas John Spykman's "America's Strategy in World Politics" and "The Geography of the Peace," and Samuel Flagg Bemis' "The Latin-American Policy of the United States."

More recent publications have consisted of studies of the postwar relations of the great powers. They are: William T. R. Fox's "The Super-Powers," David Nelson Rowe's "China among the Powers," and Percy E. Corbett's "Britain: Partner for Peace."

The most recent volume issued was a collaborative analysis of atomic power entitled "The Absolute Weapon," written by members of the Institute and edited by Bernard Brodie.

Frederick Sherwood Dunn, Director

The
Mediterranean

ITS ROLE IN AMERICA'S FOREIGN POLICY

William Reitzel

New York

HARCOURT, BRACE AND COMPANY

Acknowledgment

It is difficult to distinguish between the help of the Associates of the Yale Institute of International Studies and the fact of the Institute's existence in making this book possible and in seeing that it kept its eye on essentials. How is the growth of an idea to be separated from the soil in which it develops? I can only thank the director, Frederick Sherwood Dunn, the Associates, and the secretarial staff in their individual capacities and in their "collectivized" form for what they have so willingly done.

WILLIAM REITZEL

Author's Note

Geographical terms are used as follows:

1) *Mediterranean, Mediterranean Region, Region,* which is taken to consist of the Sea, its littoral, and such adjacent areas as are at present economically, politically, or strategically relevant. The hinterland has been consequently expanded beyond conventional usage in some instances.

2) *Western, Eastern* are the areas lying on either side of a line drawn from the entrance of the Adriatic Sea to the western border of Tripolitania.

3) *Middle East* is the only term used for the area which extends from Egypt and the Levant eastwards to Afghanistan and northwards to the Soviet Union.

A distinction is made between notes which supplement the text and footnote references. The former are marked with symbols (*) and accompany the text. The latter are numbered consecutively for each chapter and are put at the end of the volume.

Table of Contents

The Mediterranean
ITS ROLE IN AMERICA'S
FOREIGN POLICY

I. The Scene and the Theme

UNTIL very recently the United States had no interest in the Mediterranean that it consciously asserted as vital. It is now suspected, even if not wholly believed, that such an interest exists, though what its nature may be is not clear. A variety of definitions have been put forward. The petroleum reserves of the Middle East have been called essential to national security. It is said to be important to keep the Soviet Union out of the Mediterranean. American policy in Europe claims the need for a firm strategic support in the Mediterranean. More generally, it is held that democracy must spread and communism must be checked and that the Mediterranean is one of the key areas in which to exert American influence and power to this end. None of these definitions has been accepted unreservedly by American opinion.

Their accumulated impact on opinion has built up, however, a general and somewhat uneasy feeling that the Mediterranean is linked with the future of the United States. But American judgment has no yardstick by which it can reliably measure the correctness of this conclusion. American history provides no points of reference. Traditional concepts of the Mediterranean, largely derived from the immediate past and reflecting the experience of nations other than the United States, offer easy but not necessarily correct explanations. Exaggerated estimates of such incalculable forces as atomic energy and the Communist International encourage the fluent denial of any and all preconceptions. Uncritical enthusiasm projects its hopes into a region which is not demonstrably willing to co-operate in their realization. There is, in fact, a real need for a simple examination of the situation.

The Mediterranean of recent history is a product of the geographical accident which put it between competing European powers and their eastern possessions. The continental and colonial wars of the eighteenth century gave it its present strategic significance. It became splintered as its various parts were used to weigh the balance of power on the Continent or as they became important to the operations of British sea power. More than any other single factor, the activities of British sea power broke down the centuries-old structure of the Mediterranean as a frontier zone between the Moslem and Christian worlds and set up in its place a loose construction of political fragments held together by a system of semi-colonial control.

International trade followed, and with the stabilization of the British Empire in India and the cutting of the Suez Canal the Mediterranean took on its contemporary form. In that form it was divided first of all into eastern and western sectors. The western was further subdivided by the projection of Spain, France, and Italy into North Africa. The eastern was indelibly stamped by conflicting British and Russian interests. The whole was still further divided along its historical east-west axis by a broad route of international commerce and British imperial communications. A minimum degree of political stability was imposed by Great Britain, which exercised decisive strategic control of the whole from established strongpoints along the east-west axis.

The system of authority and influence thus developed in British hands served a double purpose. It preserved the strategic unity of the Mediterranean and made the region available in support of the non-Mediterranean interests of Great Britain. It also provided the nucleus for a vast complex of British commercial, cultural, and diplomatic interests within the Mediterranean itself.

By the start of the twentieth century it was almost impossible to separate in British policy the strands of global commercial interests, imperial defense, and international influence from problems connected with assuring the internal stability of the Mediterranean. Yet two basic attitudes can be discerned in general policy. One saw the Mediterranean from without and was chiefly concerned with adjusting the region to the world-wide interests of Great Britain. The other saw the Mediterranean from within and was primarily absorbed by the detailed adjustment of its internal conflicts. Although differences frequently arose between these two points of view, they were regarded as essentially complementary.

Normally, the over-all strategic requirements of Great Britain took precedence, and the Mediterranean was steadily adapted to the external objectives of policy. It was on these grounds that conflicting British and Russian interests developed in the eastern sector of the region. Russian imperial designs had long included expansion to the south and west and could not be indifferent to the system of control and administration that Great Britain was constructing in the Middle East. Spheres of influence began to be marked out and the hinterland of the eastern Mediterranean became unnaturally expanded to include the Balkans and the Arab lands to the borders of India.

The conclusion of the first World War did not significantly modify the basic pattern of these relations in the

Mediterranean. Between the two wars, however, Italy deliberately embarked on a course of action that was designed to rearrange them. Basing her foreign policy flatly on the concept of a Mediterranean unified with reference to Italy, and asserting that the region did not admit of subdivision but historically required that hegemony be organized from within its natural limits, Italy proceeded to play almost at will on the strategic sensibilities of Great Britain and France. The collapse of this thesis under the test of war does not invalidate the acute historical and political judgment with which it was developed.

In the course of the recent war, of which destruction of Italian claims was but a minor aspect, the United States became a power in the Mediterranean. The process involved the introduction of military and economic resources on a large scale, the development of joint diplomatic action with Great Britain, and participation in the civil government of extensive areas. It also implied the acceptance of responsibilities and the development of interests.

By the end of the war, the United States was in a position of power in the Mediterranean and it was using this position to support purposes elsewhere. These purposes increased in number and importance in the months following the surrender of Germany because, in President Roosevelt's words, "The people of the Nation want their Government to act, and not merely to talk, whenever and wherever there is a threat to world peace." [1] The borders of the Mediterranean offered plenty of incidents prejudicial to peace, and American policy used American power to check these threats.

In exact correspondence with the degree to which policy based itself upon a position in the Mediterranean, the United States was obliged to develop an interest in the internal stability of the region. This correspondence began, of course, the moment American forces landed in North Africa, but has grown since that time to the status of an important factor in the conduct of American foreign relations. There is no present sign that it will become less important.

In the course of five years, the objectives which demanded that this correspondence be carefully maintained have shifted. The first objectives were those set by the needs of military operations. These were gradually replaced by the need to exert American influence on the continent of Europe. The present objectives are dictated by the need to check the disintegration of the European system. This objective is usually stated in an oversimplified form as an intention to contain the Soviet Union and to resist the spread of communism.

With aims in a state of flux and methods confused by readjustments in the machinery of government, it is not surprising that the relations of the United States with the Mediterranean region have been without the guidance of a comprehensive and consistent purpose. It is now clearly desirable to work out the whole story and to try to pin down its meaning. The course of events from the start to the statement of the Truman Doctrine needs orderly presentation in the larger context of history and contemporary power relations. Finally, since it is the national interest that is in question, it is desirable to attempt to define the nature of that interest and to examine the general conditions that American policy must satisfy if its participation in Mediterranean affairs is to serve and not to frustrate national aims.

II. The American Past

BEFORE 1942, tradition kept the United States from officially developing anything even remotely like a national interest in the Mediterranean region. Individual Americans, pursuing their private ends, came and went; but their government limited itself, and was expected to limit itself, to protecting their rights. From the time of the negotiations with the Barbary Beys to negotiations with the Vichy government for supplying North Africa there runs an essential principle of non-intervention. This principle was never more succinctly put than by the Department of State in 1912: "Following the traditional American foreign policy, which forbids participation by the United States in the settlement of political questions which are entirely European in their scope, the Government must refrain from any expression of opinion." [1]

Whether or not this was an adequate basis for the conduct of foreign relations is a matter for partisan debate. That it was cut exactly to the measure of American interests as understood by Americans is a matter of historical record. Theodore Roosevelt's attempt at Algeciras to take a more positive line was reluctantly accepted and firmly condemned by the Senate as a step "taken without purpose to depart from the traditional American foreign policy." President Wilson's request for authority to assume a mandate for Armenia was rejected because of the danger of becoming involved in the conflicts of European diplomacy.* The administrators of the national interest hewed consistently to this line, and if the executive arm appeared ever to falter, the legislative arm was ready to apply the rod.

Direct participation in European affairs between 1918 and 1923 brought no relaxation of the principle. The Department of State noted, in connection with a proposal to set up an International Board of Control for the Dardanelles, that this would merely "provide an opportunity for busybodies and be a constant source of irritation." It also said, when American missionaries protested their treatment in Morocco, that while reluctant to permit such things without protest, it was "equally reluctant to raise an issue so pregnant with possible difficulties. . . ." And, in reply to a British proposal for a joint reproof to Bulgaria, the American Ambassador in Sofia was told "scrupulously [to] refrain from . . . making representations or giving advice. . . ." He was, however, given liberty to express "this country's profound interest in the development of a better understanding among nations." [2]

While thus guarding against entanglement, the United States kept a zealous foot in the "Open Door." It always spoke with a surer voice in the rough and tumble of international commerce. Under the clear guidance of domestic pressures, it worked its way without difficulty through negotiations about the oil resources of the Middle East. And, in a much less important situation, the Greek government was sharply told that the United States while "most anxious not

* Admiral Bristol, the American High Commissioner for Turkey in 1919, reporting on this matter, said coldly that nationally there was no such thing as Armenia, and that to assume the existence in this case of a principle of self-determination would only serve to draw the United States into the politics of the Middle East.

See "U.S. Naval Detachment in Turkish Waters," *Administrative Service Reference Reports, No. 2*, Navy Department, 1943, pp. 2, 7.

to give the impression that it seeks . . . more than equal opportunity . . . considers the . . . failure to accord Durham a radio contract as creating an obligation of granting a telephone concession to the International Telephone and Telegraph Corporation." [3]

But, though the internationalism proposed by President Wilson had been rejected, American interests seemed to require a more consistent participation in international affairs than ever before. The resources of traditional methods were strained and considerable ingenuity was needed to fit hallowed principles to unregenerate fact. Individual officials often felt that the method was out of gear with reality and that the channels of diplomatic action were becoming clogged with elaborate circumlocutions.* The difficulties were frequently illustrated.

When Admiral Bullard was sent to the Adriatic in 1918 with instructions "to collaborate with his colleagues in overseeing the surrender of Austrian vessels," this safe guidance was only distantly related to the actual circumstances which confronted him. Within two months his duties had broadened to the extent that he was engaged in frustrating Italian expansion at the expense of Yugoslavia. At some point in this development his instructions were changed to: ". . . be guided by the general principles laid down by the President. . . . Our good offices [are to] be used to maintain order and assist local government . . . in adjusting matters local and international as they arise." [4] The Admiral and his successors grew into military governors with wide unspecified powers.

* See Ambassador Child's letter to the Secretary of State concerning the Lausanne Conference, and the Secretary's reply. Also, Lord Curzon's conversation with the Ambassador, in *Foreign Relations of the United States*, 1923, Vol. II, pp. 897, 890.

The need to write a Turkish treaty was a more comprehensive example of the problem.* As soon as the Conference
was proposed, the Department of State sent *aides mémoires*
to London, Paris, and Rome, saying that the United States
did not desire to take part in the final peace negotiations or to
assume responsibility for the political and territorial adjustments which might be effected; on the other hand, it did
not want to give the impression that it regarded American
interests as less entitled to consideration than those of other
powers. For the Ambassadors at these places, the Department confidentially added:

> It is appreciated . . . that it will be practically im-
> possible for the Allies to conduct negotiations without
> dealing with matters in which this Government is inter-
> ested.
> To permit the Allies to conclude their negotiations
> without an attempt to present the Department's views
> . . . would leave this Government with a *fait accompli*
> as far as relations between the Allies and the Turks were
> concerned. . . . American observers will be present
> . . . ready at any opportune or critical moment to inter-
> pose the necessary word for our protection.[5]

In spite of a growing awareness of a problem, none of
the practical difficulties encountered were sufficiently important in themselves to force a reconsideration of the basic
principle. Not only was the current of domestic opinion
strongly against revision, but there was no focusing of interests in the Mediterranean to provide the political pressure

---

* The United States had not declared war on Turkey in 1918. Its
position at Lausanne in 1923 was accordingly difficult to define. Following
the Conference, the United States government conducted separate negotiations with Turkey, but the proposed agreement became a political football
and was not ratified by the Senate. Relations were based upon a *modus
vivendi* until 1930 when a strictly commercial treaty was approved.

that would have been needed to lift the question to the level of a general debate. Traditional conviction was against any course of action that implied a long-term national interest or suggested self-perpetuating commitments. Official opinion continued to be expressed only in connection with specific incidents; official policy continued to be the local application of general principles developed for other times and other places. Diplomatic activities in the Mediterranean were thus carried out as a series of disparate operations in the name of an elevated commercial policy. The related principle of non-intervention naturally led foreign governments to conclude that the United States had no interests in the Mediterranean beyond those precisely stated. In this conclusion, the American government heartily concurred.

Though official practice might follow a line of studied indifference toward the political forces that worked in the Mediterranean, it did not mean that American opinion was without a strong set of "views" about the region. Official and public opinion consistently adopted the judgments of powers that frankly admitted and vigorously pursued vital interests there. The language and conclusions of "power politics" were adapted simultaneously with the refusal to make power commitments. In fact, American unwillingness to be entangled was frequently justified by reference to these terms. The materials of experience, by which this received opinion might conceivably have been modified into a purely American interpretation of the Mediterranean, were lacking and were not sought.

During the prelude to the recent war, these habitual modes of thought prevented the development of a new approach. Stereotyped phrases like "the life line of empire," "the path to the heart of Europe," "an outlet to warm water," "Balkanization," and "historical rights" worked so strongly and seemed so applicable that a detached and purely American judgment was virtually impossible. American thinking clung firmly to conventional attitudes acquired at second hand. This was the equipment with which the United States entered the Mediterranean in 1942.*

* It was much easier for Great Britain to go against such preconceptions than it was for the United States to believe that she had really done so. Thus, in 1936, the British government stated that the problem of maintaining an imperial life line was *not* the major issue in the Mediterranean. The real issue was to prevent the formation of a vacuum that might be filled to Great Britain's disadvantage. Yet, in 1946, Professor Morison can still write that "the British have a paramount interest in the Mediterranean because of the Suez Canal, as the United States has in the Caribbean because of the Panama Canal."

See E. Monroe, *The Mediterranean in Politics*, Oxford University Press, 1938, p. 11; S. E. Morison, *Operations in North African Waters*, Little, Brown, 1947, p. 254.

III. Invasion: 1942

THE landings in North Africa opened a new theater in more than a military sense, even though the objectives of "Operation Torch" were strictly limited to military ends.* Some thought had been given to North African economy, but in general little account was taken of the responsibilities that might develop. It was assumed that the French would carry the burden of civil administration. Diplomatic preparations were similarly limited and, at bottom, consisted of little more than a successful conspiracy. They provided no basis for the handling of subsequent political tensions.

In short, the United States approached the Mediterranean with no motive except that of using it as the base for a campaign in a war against Germany and Italy. This limited view was, however, rapidly invalidated by events. The adjustments of modern society were so delicate and the impact of modern war so comprehensive that an elaborate web of nonmilitary activities had to be organized merely to protect the military advantages gained.

Allied Force Headquarters, within days, became involved with purely civilian problems: scarcities, economic dislocations, and an internal French political struggle to control the

* The objectives, as stated by the Combined Chiefs of Staff, were:
    (a) to establish firm lodgments for continued air, sea, and ground operations;
    (b) to acquire complete control of French Morocco, Algeria, and Tunisia;
    (c) to annihilate Axis forces in the Western Desert, and to intensify air and sea operations against the Axis on the European continent.
See Morison, *op. cit.*, pp. 16, 254.

administration of the African Empire. These demanded immediate attention because they directly affected the continuing success of the military operation. Calls for help went out to American and British civilian agencies. The Lend-Lease Administrator was instructed to "extend aid." A combined Anglo-American North African Economic Board was established in December, 1942. An Office of Foreign Relief and Rehabilitation was set up and had a field staff in North Africa by early 1943.*

On the political side, after General Eisenhower reported that "Existing French sentiment in North Africa does not even remotely resemble prior calculations," [1] political advisers and special staffs were added to his Headquarters. To the military burden was joined the need to estimate and to balance the power of contending groups and the influence of competing personalities. The position was made more delicate by the obvious fact that the victorious group was certain to be in a favorable position for becoming the government of France at the end of hostilities.

The ramifying problems of what had been planned as a limited military operation called for a rapid scaling upward as well as a diversification of the force needed to make it effective. This revision, made in the course of 1943, fixed the United States as an active participant in Mediterranean affairs, and is basic to the development of the present American position in the Mediterranean.

Revisions took place in three categories of activity—the purely military, the purely civilian, and the indeterminate

* *The Seventh Quarterly Report on Lend Lease* (December, 1942), noted the purchase of $5,000,000 worth of civilian goods for shipment to North Africa and plans to expand agricultural production, improve transportation facilities, and increase the production of strategic materials for export.

field of Military Government and Civil Affairs. These categories, all coming under the immediate authority of Allied Force Headquarters and under the ultimate authority of the Combined Chiefs of Staff, were never sharply separated in concept or practice. Daily decisions, made in the catch-all name of "military necessity," permitted a degree of commitment in non-military matters that would probably not have been acceptable in any other context.

In the purely military field, whatever assumptions had been originally made of British responsibility in the Mediterranean were dropped. Limitations of both manpower and matériel made it impossible for Great Britain to mount the large-scale operations that alone promised success. A steady build-up of American power was the alternative.

The U. S. Army had committed 84,000 men to "Operation Torch." Two years later it was maintaining nearly one million men in the Mediterranean Theater. In December, 1942, when the assault phase of the landings was completed, the U. S. Navy kept only insignificant establishments in the Mediterranean; but by the end of 1944 there was the Eighth Fleet with bases at Casablanca, Oran, Bizerte, Palermo, Naples, Maddalena, and Marseille, and there were two destroyer squadrons, a considerable amphibious force, a blimp squadron, and an extended air patrol and transport commitment based on Port Lyautey.

In the purely civilian field, responsibilities and activities multiplied on a comparable scale. The United States had to meet normal imports of sugar, tea, and milk, and catch up the slack in fertilizers, spray, agricultural tools, fuel, and food. In addition it had to allot for military use—that is, for feeding labor, avoiding food riots, preventing disease, and supplying the French army—80,000 tons of flour, 6,500 of wheat, and 2,800 of potatoes.² The work of the economic, relief, and political sections of Allied Force Headquarters became so interlocked with each other and with the supply functions of the Army Service Forces that a Civil Affairs Division was established in the War Department and assigned the duty of planning the future handling of similar problems. Its first task was to prepare for the military government of Sicily and Italy.

At the time, the overriding consideration was the war, and all decisions were duly subordinated to military needs. Yet, coincidentally with military operations, the inescapable need for civil government presented itself. Nothing canceled for long the interest of the indigenous population in food, clothing, work, and some sort of social organization. This meant, in effect, that the Allied Military Command was the final authority to whom these claims were presented. No discreet formula confirming the sovereignty of other agencies could hide the fact that the Allied Command alone had access to Procurement and Allocation Boards and was able to secure shipping space.

Thus, between December, 1942, and the summer of 1943, a pattern of authority and control was hammered out in the Mediterranean. A combined military operation was shaped by events into a rough and ready form of government administered by the United States and Great Britain. Allied Force Headquarters operated with a personnel that was almost equally divided between American and British; it operated as an agency of the Combined Chiefs of Staff; and beyond that body stood the authority of the two interested governments.*

* A matter of terminology should be made clear at this point. "Combined" means an Anglo-American activity. "Joint" means an interdepart-

At the eastern end of the Mediterranean was another command, the British Middle East Command, similarly an agent of the Combined Chiefs of Staff. While this command was not a fully integrated Anglo-American activity, it did supervise the Middle East Supply Center, which was a combined Board. The work of this Board inevitably brought the eastern Mediterranean into working contact with the western Mediterranean. Co-ordination between the two theaters became increasingly necessary.

The Middle East Supply Center had been set up by Great Britain in April, 1941. It became a combined Board early in 1942. Its functions were to supervise "imports, and to some extent the production of 18 Middle East countries in order to conserve Allied shipping and resources and at the same time prevent economic break-down in this sensitive crossroads area of 70 million inhabitants by insuring that sufficient civilian supplies were available." [3]

Throughout the entire Mediterranean therefore, excepting the areas under Axis domination, the United States and Great Britain were the single controlling authority. This control was based on military force in actual position in the area, and on the ownership of essential supplies. The harshness of this reality was softened by the use of local systems of authority, and was concealed to some extent even from its administrators by being correlated with military exigencies. It is important, however, to assert its basic character as a system approximating the authority of a government, because it was in such a context that American commitments developed in the Mediterranean.

mental activity within the same government. The Combined Chiefs of Staff was an Anglo-American body. The Joint Chiefs of Staff was an American body. There was a corresponding British Joint Chiefs of Staff. This distinction held throughout the war.

The American and British contributions to this authority, and their interest in the purposes for which it was exercised, differed in kind as well as in degree. Essentially, the United States contributed the full weight of its power potential and Great Britain contributed an established system of administration, influence and experience, and a traditional position of power. This division was not intentional nor was it as absolute as here stated. The fact that American force was concentrated in the western Mediterranean and British force in the eastern, and that the Middle East was officially noted as "an area of primary British strategic responsibility," obscured the broad interplay between the material strength of the United States and the historical experience and interest of Great Britain that was so notable a feature of Anglo-American control throughout the entire Mediterranean Basin.*

The final touch, which gave this complex structure the real attributes of a government, came with the defeat of Italy. By this victory Anglo-American authority not only took over the territory and government of a defeated enemy, but was automatically obliged to fill the vacuum created in the Mediterranean region by the collapse of Italy as an effective power. In connection with this last point, the problems with which authority had to deal became increasingly diplomatic and involved genuine issues of power relations.

The defeat of Italy, though it simplified the future conduct of the war, complicated the conduct of international re-

* This interplay can be studied in the handling of Spanish affairs at one end of the Mediterranean and in the handling of Franco-Syrian crises at the other.

See Carleton Hayes, *Wartime Mission in Spain*, Macmillan, 1945; Lord Templewood, *Complacent Dictator*, Alfred A. Knopf, 1947; as well as relevant issues of the Department of State *Bulletin* for statements on Syrian affairs.

lations. From this moment, as a growing undercurrent in the Mediterranean, a conventional pattern of relations began to reassert its influence on judgment and action. This pattern, created by a century of imperial interests, economic and strategic conflicts, and by the internal tensions of the region itself, was the pattern into which Italy had vigorously inserted herself between 1930 and 1942 and from which France had, perforce, withdrawn in 1940. It was, furthermore, a pattern in which Russia had played a significant part until 1920, and a pattern to whose slightest modification Great Britain was traditionally sensitive.

A single illustration—the effort made by the French to re-establish their authority in the Levant in 1943—shows the current that was set in motion.

The background of this effort was the occupation of Syria and Lebanon by Free French and British troops in June, 1941. This operation had been accompanied by a declaration of Syrian and Lebanese independence. General de Gaulle, from London, had promptly defined this as meaning not a grant of independence, but willingness to discuss the question. Churchill, with equal promptness, contradicted him and stated, in the House of Commons, that independence would be granted without waiting for the end of the war, adding that there could be no question of France maintaining her prewar position in the Levant. The independence of Syria and Lebanon was accordingly proclaimed by General Catroux, and the two states were recognized a year later by the American government.

Nothing more happened until June, 1943, when political control was consolidated in General de Gaulle's hands in Algiers. Then, while the Allies conducted military operations against Italy, the newly devised French Committee of Na-

tional Liberation undertook to re-establish French authority
in the Levant. It began by asserting that France had a mandate from the League of Nations. This was an international
obligation from which a unilateral British decision did not
constitute release. The French Delegate General in Syria
implemented this assertion by dissolving the Lebanese Cham-
ber of Deputies, arresting the President, Prime Minister, and
other difficult officials, and by appointing a Prime Minister
of his own choosing.

Egypt, in the name of all Arabs, protested. King Ibn
Saud and the governments of Trans-Jordan and Iraq simultaneously expressed their horror to the British. General
Spears, British Minister at Beirut, whom French officials in
the Levant regarded with pathological suspicion, became the
moving spirit behind a British statement explaining the political and strategic grounds for a profound concern. The
American government sent a note to the Committee in Algiers supporting the British position.

Since these representations rested on a solid foundation of
Anglo-American authority, the Committee of National Liberation gave in, contenting itself with remarking that American power was obviously putting itself at the service of a
purely British interest.*

The detailed development and resolution of this matter
are of little importance. Its significance lies in reflecting the
persistence of traditional interests and relations in the Mediterranean area. It also reveals the ambiguity of the American position. The sole immediate concern of the United
States was the conduct of the war. The disparity between
American power in the region and any stated interests there

* This opinion was often heard by the author in the talk of French
political circles in Algiers.

was so great that decisions emerging from a combined Anglo-American authority were certain to be understood as meaning a more complete identification of American power and British interest than was in fact the case.

The United States, with only a negative tradition of non-intervention to refer to, and with no established position to defend, naturally found it difficult to formulate a course of action that would simultaneously meet the needs of the moment, avoid dangerous reflexes in domestic opinion, and not run counter to the broad and positive experience which Great Britain brought to the combined councils of the Mediterranean. Accordingly, the American government insisted more strongly than ever on the primacy of military considerations.

Official reluctance to take a fixed position with respect to the complex pattern of Mediterranean affairs was strengthened by the existence of frequently asserted convictions in American public opinion. The tendency to see British and French actions as signs of an oppressive and outmoded imperialism, the belief that Balkan resistance groups were politically as well as militarily liberating movements, the firm judgment against General Franco's regime in Spain, the feeling that the Arab world was being exploited against its will as an economic colony, the assumption that Italy was a liberated nation and not a defeated enemy inhibited the development of clear lines of action.* In these circumstances it was impossible for the American government quickly to formulate a positive policy to which its representatives could

* In the case of Spain, the desire of the American military authorities for a policy that would preserve internal calm had to be continually balanced against a public opinion pressing for the punishment of a regime that was held to be collaborationist and totalitarian. The practical difficulties are amply illustrated in Ambassador Hayes' volume cited earlier.

refer with assurance. The general principles of the Atlantic Charter and the Declaration of the United Nations, as the only existing points of reference, offered dim broad clues, not effective guidance.

For these reasons the problem of Italy led to a genuine dilemma. It called for action in order to maintain the impetus of military success; but action could not be limited in its consequences. Immediate military considerations and longer term political and social tensions could not be kept in watertight compartments. They became irretrievably mixed.

Though defeated, Italy possessed a recognized government under Marshal Badoglio; though signatory of an armistice acknowledging defeat, Italy was admitted to the status of a cobelligerent; though socially disintegrated and anxious only for peace, Italy remained an active region of battle. Furthermore, since her collapse was more complete than had been anticipated, the first practical requirement was to hold Italy together as a going concern. Finally, as the first member of the Axis to be conquered, her surrender raised fundamental questions of tripartite principle and procedure for the United States, Great Britain, and Soviet Russia. It also encouraged the Mediterranean governments-in-exile to stake out claims against a defeated enemy and emboldened them to reassert their traditional interests in an area where that enemy had been a dominating force for two decades.

These questions were discussed at Moscow in October, 1943, by Hull, Eden, and Molotov. The agreements there reached superimposed an additional complication by obligating the United States and Great Britain to carry out a tripartite policy with respect to Italy. The essential principle of this policy was "that Fascism and all its evil influences and emanations shall be utterly destroyed and that the Italian people shall be given every opportunity to establish governmental and other institutions based upon democratic principles." [4]

This obligation, along with all other problems, was translated into two pieces of machinery—the Allied Control Commission for Italy (an Anglo-American body under the presidency of the Allied Theater Commander) and the Advisory Council for Italy (a body with American, British, Russian, and French—and later Yugoslav and Greek— members). The former supervised the execution of the terms of the armistice and acted in an advisory capacity with the Italian government on matters of military, economic, and civilian administration. The latter dealt with day-to-day questions, other than military operations, and made recommendations designed to co-ordinate Allied policy with respect to Italy. [5]

In practice, it was the Control Commission and not the Advisory Council that was the effective authority. It was the body that handled the real and pressing problems of the internal life of Italy, and it was the body which was responsible for making Italy useful to the war effort. The Advisory Council became a more or less inoperative symbol of tripartite relations. The essential point was that the Control Commission, linked with the authority of Allied Force Headquarters, was the executive arm in Italy of that combined Anglo-American power which ultimately stood for government in the Mediterranean.

IV. The Italian Problem: 1943

IT was inevitable that Italy should become the central theme of developments in the Mediterranean after 1943. The knocking out of one of the major elements of the pre-war pattern of the region could only serve to introduce the general problem of political adjustment. In addition, it opened the way for the expression of a reawakened Russian interest. Thus, quite aside from the problems of the internal reorganization of Italy, issues appeared in connection with Italy's position as a Mediterranean nation and in connection with Italy's strategic value as a factor in great power relations. The simplest problem could, with some show of historical reason, suggest immense consequences.

The United States brought only a very generalized policy to the handling of the problems thus presented. Looking back on the efforts to apply these generalizations, it can be seen more clearly than was possible at the time that America had entered on a new and unexpected phase in the history of its foreign relations. It had reached a position of strength and influence in the Mediterranean; and, on the basis of that position, undertook decisions which were intended to be of limited application to Italy. Italy, however, was not an isolated phenomenon; it was a central point from which the consequences of decisions spread in widening circles. The American government, as soon as it began to implement a limited policy for Italy, found itself engaged in working out solutions to a large complex of unanticipated issues.

This complex consisted of problems which arranged themselves at various levels of importance and intensity, yet were so interrelated that any one of them was likely to condition judgment of the whole. There was a tripartite aspect, involving the procedures by which one or more members of the wartime coalition were to act on behalf of all. There was an Anglo-American aspect, involving differences of essential attitude between the British and American governments. There was an Italian aspect, involving the political character of the revived Italian nation. There was a Mediterranean aspect, involving the claims of Yugoslavia, Greece, and France against a defeated enemy, and involving simultaneously the relations of a new and democratic Italy with neighbors against whom the old fascist Italy had waged an unsuccessful war. And, finally, there was a Russian aspect, involving the possible return of Russian influence to a region in which that influence had not been exerted for over thirty years.

For Great Britain, the defeat of Italy was a different category of victory than for the United States. To the former, it was a period put to fifteen years of political confusion and strategic anxieties; it was the elimination of a local rival who had come dangerously close to making good his boasts. It was the essential first and major step in the process of restoring a Mediterranean position that had seriously deteriorated. If victory created problems, it also provided practical opportunities.

To the United States, the defeat of Italy was primarily a stage in the war against Germany. It was a defeat administered more in sorrow than in anger. It was vaguely felt that Italy had been liberated and that, generally speaking, she was to be encouraged to return to her pre-fascist traditions. If victory presented problems, they were to be dealt with rapidly and practically in order to get on to the next stage of the war.

The contradictions implicit in these two approaches did not develop until after the signing of the Italian armistice in September, 1943, and did not become difficult until after the Moscow Agreement of October. Then, under the tri-partite injunction to give "the Italian people every oppor-tunity to establish governmental and other institutions based upon democratic principles," a wilderness of confus-ing interpretations began to grow up.* The wilderness was made even more impenetrable by the total disorganization of Italian life which the Allied occupation revealed, and which demanded emergency action.

Events, in this respect, moved with great speed, and were consistently in advance of policy. The rate of importation for civilian supplies rose until it was clearly approximating the total consumer goods needed for civilian existence. The Al-lied Control Commission began a full-scale study of the means of reviving Italian production. The military require-

* It is more important to grasp the opposing points of view than it is to report detailed disagreements. The English found it hard to overlook the actual damage done by Italy and were skeptical of Italian democracy. The Americans were overeager to shift from being conquerors to being liberators, and were optimistic about Italian democracy. British observers reported that the complete suppression of fascist organizations would work practical hardships, that the Italian nature was not inclined to democratic principles and methods, and that British and American opinion was mis-informed about the appeal of democratic institutions in the face of hunger and economic chaos. Official American opinion, backed by a vocal public feeling, maintained that the United States was committed to assuring Italian freedom, and refused to accept Churchill's view that a more demo-cratic government would not be as helpful to the Allies as a deliberate bolstering of the undemocratic Badoglio regime. The description of these oppositions as "soft" and "hard" is an unrealistic simplification of the actual situation in Italy and of the actions that were taken to deal with it.

ment of a stable line of communications became identified with the political obligation to create a stable foundation for democratic institutions. But comprehensive solutions were prevented not only by the facts of limited supplies and shipping space, but equally by such psychological facts as the British reluctance to go beyond basic minimums in relief and rehabilitation.

Compromise was ultimately forced by the drawing out of the Italian campaign and even more significantly by the appearance of the Soviet Union as an interested party. In the face of these facts, the first of which worked strongly on American official opinion and the second of which worked strongly on British official opinion, Anglo-American policy with respect to the internal condition of Italy became increasingly unified.

An equal uniformity could not, however, be reached with respect to other problems that came up in the Mediterranean in the wake of the Italian collapse. The appearance of the Soviet Union as a relevant factor in these problems increased the difficulty of co-ordinating American and British views. A simple chronology of events is enough to suggest the nature and extent of the issues.

Early in December, 1943, the Yugoslav partisan, Tito, announced the establishment of a Provisional Government of National Liberation. When, however, he sent representatives to Cairo to consult with King Peter's government-in-exile, they were not received. In January, 1944, the Soviet Union found that it could not conclude a pact of mutual assistance with the Yugoslav government-in-exile. In April, Tito's representatives were consulting in Moscow. At the end of the same month, a Greek Resistance Group, E.A.M., also set up a Provisional Government, and there was a mutiny in the Greek forces stationed at Alexandria.*

In British Mediterranean eyes, this sequence could only add up to an old formula—Russia was interested in coming back into the Mediterranean scene and was putting a finger into every available pie. She was pulling Yugoslavia into a Russian orbit. She was testing the general British position by fomenting discords between partisans and governments-in-exile. She was prejudicing future settlements well in advance. The implications of these activities were difficult to deal with in the early stages of their unfolding.

For one thing, since authoritative control in the Mediterranean rested on Anglo-American power, effective action had to be combined action, and this required American agreement. Yet these evidences of Russian pressure, no matter how valid they seemed in the British judgment, did not carry equal conviction to Americans. American public opinion was inclined to see an anti-royalist partisan as probably more democratic than a royalist one and, in any case, felt that a British imperial interest was not in itself a good reason for lending American support to its maintenance. In addition, official American policy, strongly supported by this same public opinion, was committed to tripartite solutions during the war and to preparing the ground for internationally agreed solutions after the war. Decisions, if they appeared

---

* At Moscow, in October, 1943, when Great Britain presented a memorandum on the Balkans in which concern was expressed at the growth of conflict between partisan and exiled governments, Molotov declined to discuss it or to be interested in co-ordinating policy. At Teheran, in December, he refused to join the United States and Great Britain in a statement to the Greek partisans, saying that he did not have an accurate knowledge of the situation in Greece. By January 15, 1944, however, the Soviet newspaper *War and the Working Classes* had enough background to attack Zervas, the leader of the Greek Royalist partisans, and to accuse the Greek Information Office in Cairo of disrupting tripartite unity.

to be made in terms of purely British interests, could not be readily reconciled with such commitments.

The degree of American consent that would allow coherent combined action could not be obtained without considerable modification of both British and American attitudes. That these modifications were actually made is shown by the comparative uniformity that continued to mark the decisions of Allied Force Headquarters; but that they were made reluctantly is indicated by the backing and filling of both governments as they felt their way toward realistic compromises. Necessity, however, was on the side of compromise and frequently produced practical accord on the spot before agreement was reached at higher governmental levels.*

In the face of this necessity, the internal problems of Italy could not be settled as if they bore no relation to the general problems of the Mediterranean. The relationship was denied, resisted, and ignored; but at last policy had to accept the fact. The process was slow, and many of its stages were encompassed hesitatingly by the American government. The formulation of an American position, adequate to the total situation and yet free from those precise commitments that spelt political controversy at home or malicious misinterpretation abroad, was an almost impossible task.

* A contributing factor in this respect was a change in the responsibilities assigned to Allied Force Headquarters. Early in 1944 a redefinition of military theaters of operation removed the Balkans and Yugoslavia from the Middle East Command and gave them to Allied Force Headquarters. Only Greece was retained in the Middle Eastern Theater. In consequence, the responsibilities and interests of these two Commands were even more closely linked than before and a detailed co-ordination of their activities became a matter of course. In addition, since Allied Force Headquarters was responsible for maintaining Italian economy and administering Italian affairs, it was sensitive to the ultimate position of Italy in the Mediterranean.

The first push toward such a position was given by the fact that the scale of rehabilitation in Italy had to be enormously expanded if Italy was to take part effectively in the war. This obvious need was consonant with the democratic and humanitarian urges of American public feeling, and fitted, furthermore, the obligation to develop democratic institutions in Italy.

The Allied Control Commission was responsible for planning and administering the reorganization of Italian economy. Its means, however, bore no relation to the immensity of the task. Early in 1944 a crisis could be anticipated. It was reported to Washington that Italy was on the verge of starvation and chaos, and that a policy was needed that would prevent such a development. Failure, it was added, would benefit no one but the Italian Communists. The proposals for meeting it were so comprehensive that they called for a basic revision of policy and practice. The most essential revision called for was that the United States and Great Britain should jointly agree to assume full responsibility for the stability of Italy as a nation. The resulting discussions were protracted and revealed the need for considerable compromise on the British part and extensive commitment on the American. In September, 1944, Roosevelt and Churchill made the desired statement.

It consisted of two parts: a political decision that an increasing measure of control would be gradually handed over to Italian administration; and an economic decision that first steps would be taken toward the reconstruction of Italian economy, the restoration of power systems, railways, motor transport, and other communications, and the assignment of engineers, technicians, and industrial experts.[1] In addition, the Council of UNRRA, meeting shortly afterward at

Montreal, authorized, as requested by the United States and Great Britain, a limited relief program of $50,000,000, thus removing Italy from its list as an enemy country.

Official American publicity concerning this decision was stabilized around the theme: ". . . if, by our providing help at this critical period, Italy can achieve economic and political conditions favorable to the development of democratic institutions and policies . . . our investment in effort and money may be well worth while." [2] The action was also presented as a logical step in the general policy of preventing chaos in Europe, referring to an earlier statement by the Secretary of State to the effect that "It is essential that we and our Allies establish the controls necessary to bring order out of this chaos as rapidly as possible . . . a stable Europe should be an immediate objective of allied policy." [3] For the British part, Churchill, subsequent to a talk with Stalin and during a visit to Rome, spoke of the Seven Points of Freedom, and markedly included Italy as a partaker. In addition, official publicity was instructed to present the matter as a natural development from the Italian willingness to share the burden of the war and not as a change of Anglo-American policy.

Since the actual methods of carrying out this decision were financial and economic, the major burden fell to the United States, and Italy and its internal problems became a special American concern. Though conscious interest was thus precisely limited, the policy opened the way for related external problems to come flooding in. If it was agreed to rehabilitate Italy, the immediate question arose—to what end? The official answer, "to achieve economic and political conditions favorable to the development of democratic institutions and policies," was no daily practical guide. Policy for

Italy was not an abstraction. It faced such considerations as the position of the Communist Party in Italian politics, the relations between Italy and the Yugoslavia of Tito, the control of Italy's strategically placed colonies, the strategic position of Italy in the Mediterranean. At Allied Force Headquarters and in the Allied Control Commission a directive to rehabilitate Italy could only be understood to mean rehabilitation in the image of the Western democracies and in a form compatible with the estimated interests of those democracies.*

This natural interpretation was supported and strengthened by the deepening instability of the general Mediterranean situation. The chronology begun earlier can be completed here for the year 1944. In September the Soviet Union demanded concessions in Iran. Also in September came the Soviet-written armistices with Rumania and Bulgaria, followed in October by Tito's repudiation of his obligations to Great Britain and the United States. In November Vishinsky intervened in Rumanian internal affairs and secured a new government, and in December the formation of an autonomous Macedonian government was announced. The year closed with the Greek civil war.

Against the background of these events it appeared certain that the defeat of Italy had not caused a greater vacuum in the Mediterranean simply because Anglo-American power had instantaneously flowed in. But, since permanent occupation by these nations was out of the question, it was necessary to anticipate and guard against the situation that would exist when Anglo-American power was withdrawn. The ob-

* As a sign of the times, *Newsweek*, October 9, 1944, explained the Roosevelt-Churchill statement as indicating "a growing concern with the mounting prestige of the USSR, and . . . an effort to halt the drift towards communism."

vious conclusion was that Italy herself should be made ready for that moment.

An implicit objective of Allied policy was accordingly shaped. The "development of democratic institutions" became less of a verbal formula and more of a positive intention to construct a system securely tied by interest to the West. It is not necessary to prove that such an aim was officially envisaged by the American government. It is only necessary to note that the rehabilitation of Italy was begun under conditions which inevitably pushed policy decisions in this direction. A limited American policy was open to influences that broadened its consequences in ways not originally foreseen. As Soviet pressure seemed to accumulate, a policy that had been devised solely for Italy tended more and more to accommodate itself to the forces and interests that worked generally in the Mediterranean region.

V. Spheres of Influence: 1944

TO appreciate the atmosphere in which Italian problems were presented and in which action decisions were taken during 1944, it is necessary to go back and look at the concurrent development of a wider range of Mediterranean situations. These have been selected for their illustrative value, and the list is not complete. The following external considerations were involved in each of these situations: the necessity of maintaining the operational unity of the Anglo-American military command; the value of maintaining Anglo-American authority in the region; an overriding policy of tripartite collaboration; and the reappearance of a stereotyped Anglo-Russian conflict.

The influence of these considerations gave a particular significance to questions concerning Italy, Yugoslavia, and Greece, and made it difficult to limit the answers to the specific bodies of fact involved. There invariably remained the apprehension that some remote but important consequence, affecting a future interest or position, had been ignored. British judgment was especially sensitive to this possibility, and rightly so from a British point of view since Great Britain's ultimate power in the Mediterranean was concerned at every step.

In the case of both Yugoslavia and Greece, the position of Great Britain was delicate in 1944. Both countries had governments-in-exile which had placed their available resources under British command and which worked under agreements with the British government. The British commitment was clear, and the desirability of restoring these governments and of anchoring them in public estimation seemed self-evident. The question of their representative character was not one to be lightly raised.

Such questions were raised, however, in the course of 1944. In Greece and Yugoslavia partisan movements developed which entered into controversy with their governments-in-exile. In the favorable interpretation, this antagonism was a movement of liberal opinion against royalist groups. In the unfavorable interpretation, it was a doctrinaire communism encouraged and guided by Soviet Russia.

In Yugoslavia Tito built up an organization with wide political claims. In Greece military effectiveness became concentrated in the hands of E.A.M. (the National Liberation Front) and E.L.A.S. (the National People's Liberation Army). Both organizations were beyond the control of their respective governments-in-exile and both lent themselves to the suspicion that they were more concerned to establish themselves as future governments than to serve the operational plans of Allied Force Headquarters and the interests of exiled leaders. In consequence, the possibility of civil war had to be taken into serious account: in Yugoslavia between Tito and Mikailovich; in Greece between E.L.A.S. and E.D.E.S. (the Greek Democratic National League).

The situation was felt out in the early months of 1944, but without any positive conclusions being reached. British missions, American observers, interested pressures of every kind, and the silent ambiguity of Soviet policy thoroughly confused the practical decisions that had to be made. Reports were contradictory, and the degree to which preconceived opinion colored or substituted for fact was great. Decision tended to be pushed to the highest levels of the British and American governments for final action.

At those levels, agreement was almost impossible. The official American view was that all commitments which prejudiced postwar political settlements were to be avoided. The United States, accordingly, concentrated on estimating military value and called for the unification of all partisan groups in a common resistance.* The official Soviet position was that the Soviet Union did not have sufficient information to make an official decision. The probable direction of its inactivity was, nevertheless, suggested by the fact that differences had been developed between the Soviet Union and the Polish government-in-exile, and that Soviet propaganda had introduced the phrase "reactionary remnants" to describe exiled political figures.†

The British position could not, in contrast, be developed in terms of wait-and-see. Large consequences hung upon the decision; and decision had to be based on searching for a balance between what was justifiable to defeat the Germans and what would be inexcusable if measured by the historic British interest in the Mediterranean. The natural compromise of acting as a counsellor in a domestic dispute seemed, at first, to be successful. At Beirut in May, 1944, the British

* "Our policy has been to endeavor to bring . . . elements into sufficient harmony so that they can make a common front against a common enemy. We are, meanwhile, cooperating in furnishing arms and supplies to all Yugoslavs who are fighting the Germans."—Department of State *Bulletin*, April 15, 1944, Vol. X, No. 251, p. 343.

† From this, the American government concluded that the U.S.S.R. was playing a waiting game and would make a satisfactory deal with chosen partisan groups after the British had burnt their fingers. It was, therefore, more than ever necessary for the United States to remain detached and uncommitted. This resulted, in effect, in a series of vague generalizations whose unreality grew in direct proportion to the intensity of the issues they were designed to restrain.

government hammered out an accord for all Greek parties and resistance groups, and in August it secured a similar agreement between Tito and M. Subasich, the latter acting for the Yugoslav government-in-exile.

But neither of these accords stood up to the strain of opportunities to improve political positions. American detachment and Soviet elusiveness enabled the disputants to reassert their intransigence whenever it seemed fitting and useful to do so. And, as a by-product of Allied secret operations in the Balkans, the real balance of strength within both Yugoslavia and Greece was altered in favor of Tito and E.L.A.S. by their being chosen as recipients for arms and equipment. This gradual concentration of resources did not induce a spirit of compromise in the beneficiaries.

However, in mid-1944 both situations appeared to have been stabilized in a way that preserved basic commitments to the governments-in-exile, that guaranteed a free expression of the public will at a suitable future date, and that set the stage militarily for unified partisan activity at the time German control began to weaken. The laborious and irritating negotiations that led to these conclusions were conducted by the British without official American support and without official Soviet opposition. In so far, however, as Anglo-American military authorities in the Mediterranean were concerned in their outcome, they were tacitly underwritten by the United States on the grounds that they were of practical value to the war effort and yet did not harden the political situation by positive commitments to groups or persons.

In September, 1944, when the Germans began to withdraw from Greece and Yugoslavia, these paper hopes were destroyed. Contrary to expectations and plans, the German withdrawals were carried out in good order. Prepared partisan activities were either highly unsuccessful or conspicuously unexecuted. Tito and E.L.A.S. sat tight on their equipment or employed their strength to better their positions vis-à-vis competing partisan groups. At the same time the Red Army moved into Rumania and Bulgaria, and the junction of Soviet and Yugoslav forces could be anticipated.* Meanwhile, Anglo-American forces were still fighting Germans in northern Italy on a line that ran from Genoa to Ravenna, and the Middle East Command, partly from shorthandedness and partly from policy, had landed only a token liberation force in Greece. In a very short space of time the distribution of armed force and the possible distribution of political power along the Balkan shore of the Mediterranean was altered beyond recognition and calculation.

As part of the dissolving and rearranging picture, the movement of the Red Army into the Balkans must be mentioned. In July, 1944, the Rumanian government had sent representatives to Cairo to propose an armistice. The Soviet government was informed of their proposals and professed its dissatisfaction. Negotiations were broken off. In August the Red Army entered Rumania and a silence fell over both military operations and Rumanian affairs. Out of this silence, at the end of the month, came the news of an armistice signed by Marshal Malinovski. This unilateral document was protested by the United States and Great Britain and, after discussions in Moscow, reappeared as a tripartite armistice with an added paragraph setting up an Allied Control Commission and a notation, ex post facto, that Malinovski had

* Belgrade was liberated by joint Red Army-Partisan action on October 20. Tito conferred with Stalin in Moscow the following day.

been authorized to act in the name of the United Nations.*

Meanwhile, Bulgarian delegates had arrived in Cairo to seek terms. This procedure was more correct than that followed by the Rumanians, for Bulgaria and the Soviet Union were not at war. Again the Soviet Union was informed of the development; but while negotiations were in progress, the Soviet Union accused Bulgaria of aiding the Germans and on September 5 declared war on the government whose representatives were in Cairo. The following day a new Bulgarian government was formed and negotiations switched from Cairo to Red Army Headquarters. Five days later an armistice was signed between Bulgaria and the Soviet Union. This document, like the Rumanian one, underwent tripartite rewording and reappeared as a tripartite armistice at the end of October.

As reports began to come in of these proceedings, a picture with Machiavellian undertones was inevitably produced. Its significance was most strongly and immediately felt in the combined Anglo-American agencies in the Mediterranean. Particularly in the British sections of those agencies was it assumed that the Soviet Union, behind a screen of tripartite terminology, was engaging in the strategic moves traditional to the region. The feeling that a familiar pattern of Mediterranean relations was being reshaped can at least be understood. The liberation of Yugoslavia had renewed Yugoslav-Italian antagonisms in Venezia Giulia and the Adriatic. The liberation of Greece had revived Greco-Italian antagonisms

* The American government issued a statement to the effect that it had taken part at all stages of the negotiations and drew the dangerous analogy that the document had been presented by the Soviet Marshal in accordance with the procedure followed by General Eisenhower at the time of the Italian surrender.—Department of State *Bulletin*, October 22, 1944, Vol. XI, No. 278, p. 453.

in the Dodecanese; and the defeat of Bulgaria had reopened rather than settled the problem of the Macedonian border and a port on the Aegean. And, as a general backdrop, Tito raised the banner of a Balkan Federation, and the Soviet Union supplied a two-pronged ideological weapon of slavism and communism.

Once this pattern of interpretation was established, it provided a frame of reference for new situations and became a simplified guide to policy and action. The inevitable focus was the Soviet Union. The development of such an "on guard" attitude was contrary to official policies of tripartite collaboration. Its spread was accordingly unequal and met with powerful checks in those official circles that were removed from the urgency of Mediterranean events. It met with further resistance in British and American public feeling, both of which had been conditioned to a different view of Soviet participation in the war and in the peace.

VI. American Reluctance: 1944

THE most significant differences developed between Washington and London in this respect. Washington resisted what it took to be the revival of a power contest between Great Britain and Russia, arguing that it was prejudicial to the tripartite solution of problems in other areas of international importance. In particular, it might disturb the deliberations of the European Advisory Council, currently sitting in London on problems connected with the surrender and control of Germany.

The uncertainties introduced by American insistence on this point deepened the British sense of urgency, and at the end of October Churchill and Eden went to Moscow. The nature of their conversations with Stalin was not revealed until the following January when Churchill reported in Parliament that "Recently Bulgaria and Rumania have passed under control of the Soviet military authorities and Russian-controlled armies are in direct contact with Yugoslavia. As we feared that there might be misunderstanding and contrary policies between us and the Soviet Govt. . . . an understanding . . . [was reached] by which our two countries pursue a joint policy in these regions. . . . This agreement raised no question of division of territory or spheres of interest. . . . It arrived only at the avoidance . . . of friction. . . ."[1]

This meeting gave rise to rumors which momentarily exacerbated Anglo-American relations without perceptibly increasing tripartite collaboration. Churchill's earlier proposal of an Anglo-American invasion of the Balkans was recalled, and it was asserted that he had made a unilateral move toward the same strategic end—the protection of the British position in Greece and the Middle East—and that he had sacrificed the Balkans to gain his purpose.* The real importance of the meeting, however, lies not in the precise ground covered, but in the fact that the American government took occasion to disassociate itself specifically from this unilateral activity on the part of Great Britain. The combined Psychological Warfare Operation in the Balkans was split into separate American and British sections; and the Office of War Information withdrew from the combined planning of an Anglo-American Information Service for Greece. Separation was not pushed beyond this point however.

An implicit contradiction continued to mark the American position. The concern of the United States for tripartite unity on a world scale was practically denied by the maintenance of combined Anglo-American agencies in the Mediterranean. Even if the operation of these agencies became indecisive at crucial moments, their mere existence was enough to feed Soviet suspicions. For wherever the Soviet Union and Great Britain met in the region, the power of the United States was the skeleton at the conference.

It is not certain what practical benefits Great Britain hoped for from the conversations of Churchill and Stalin. Whatever they may have been, they could not be achieved, for internal

---

* A characteristic version of these assertions can be found in Denner, *Trouble Zone*, Ziff-Davis, 1945, p. 96, where it is said Rumania and Bulgaria were recognized as within a Russian "sphere of influence," Greece as within a British; that a compromise on Yugoslavia and the Adriatic was rejected by Stalin; and that these arrangements were confirmed at Yalta. The full text of the Yalta Agreement, released by the State Department March 25, 1947, shows no such confirmation.

dissensions in Greece moved rapidly on toward civil war and prevented all efforts at a general stabilization. When a date was set in November for the final dissolution of all Greek resistance forces, E.A.M., instead of responding to the government's appeal, made the occasion a test of strength. Civil war broke out and was only brought under temporary control by the arrival of British reinforcements from Italy.

The position of the British government was extremely difficult. The Soviet Union was embarrassingly impeccable in avoiding contacts with the Greek Communists who directed the operations of E.A.M. In marked contrast with the tone of the American press, the Moscow Radio uttered no criticism of British efforts to re-establish order.* More embarrassingly still, the American government, under pressure from a public opinion whose press invoked the bogy of a deep-dyed reactionary British imperialism, pointedly withdrew even its moral support from Great Britain. As Churchill remarked two years later in commenting on the Truman Doctrine, "We felt at that time, like Mr. Dean Acheson now, . . . that a 'Communist-dominated Government in Greece would be dangerous to British security.' . . . I was much scolded by . . . progressive organs and elements of opinion. . . . The attitude of the State Department was sourly critical. . . . Even President Roosevelt, whom I had kept constantly informed about our Greek policy, remained silent. . . ." [2]

To top the situation off, the British government ran into

* The Yugoslav Radio Belgrade, however, had a field day in this respect; and in addition, irredentist groups of Bulgars, Yugoslavs, Albanians, and Macedonians mixed into the guerrilla activities of E.A.M. Furthermore, the Soviet Union could rely on Moscow-trained leaders among the partisans to apply the letter of the Communist textbook without direct guidance.

See W. H. McNeill, *The Greek Dilemma*, Lippincott, 1947, p. 145.

domestic opposition. This came not only from opinion on the Left but from a surprisingly large and vocal middle group that suddenly saw the situation as a dismal revival of an old game. The Labour Party, pressed by its doctrinaire elements, grew restive within the coalition. None of these oppositions became coherent enough to constitute a political danger to the Churchill government, but their existence was sufficient to inhibit effective action. British policy in Greece was obliged to fall back on compromises that were so inadequate that, less than a year later, when the Labour Party took up the burden, it found itself dealing with a situation that was as unresolved as ever.

But the important consequence of these events, as far as the position of the United States in the Mediterranean is concerned, is to be found in the immediate reactions set up in Italy. There the United States had defined an interest, had accepted a responsibility, and had publicized its commitment. Long-range strategic and political factors were baldly introduced into the thinking of the combined agencies that were responsible for Italy in the present and for the Italy of the future. Slowly but surely, and at times almost in contradiction of its other policy statements, the United States developed in Italy a course of action whose objective came to be more and more definable as the shoring up of a bulwark against ideological and strategic encroachments on the part of communism and Soviet Russia.

Thus, when Great Britain and America finally began to implement a joint and uniform policy of Italian rehabilitation at the end of 1944, their conception of its purposes and values was as much conditioned by external circumstances as by Italian needs. This uniformity, though certainly a positive fact in the long run, suffered occasional setbacks in the short. These were the natural results of being obliged to exert more pronounced pressures on the unstable balance of Italian political parties than had been planned. But these differences quickly blew themselves out as teacup storms. The London *Times* accurately stated the case when it noted that "One thing is certain, and that is that Great Britain and the United States, . . . are bound to take a hand in shaping events in that country, whether they want to or not." [8]

In fact, from the moment when Rome was freed in June, 1944, and the "interim" government of Marshal Badoglio resigned, the course of Italian politics became an important object of interest to the Control Commission, Allied Force Headquarters, and the British and American governments. The basic responsibility of the Control Commission in this respect was to cushion the future against the unrestrained play of party feeling; and its ultimate right of veto, even when unexercised, was a powerful factor in giving direction to political activities. Bonomi, in July, was able to secure agreement among competitors for power by pointing out that no one of them would be acceptable to the Control Commission if he appeared as the sole claimant to political authority.

Though this was the practical working compromise between Allied interests and Italian aspirations, it was an unstable compromise at best. The diplomatic recognition of Italy by the Soviet Union, in the spring of 1944, complicated the handling of a revived Italian communism. In addition, and in accordance with the Tripartite Declaration that gave Italy the right to choose her own government, it was inevitable that Italian political parties should press against the limitations imposed by the armistice and the Control Commission. It was equally inevitable that the Control Commission should resist such pressure.

Events external to Italy, to which must be added the shift of the major military effort against Germany to northern Europe, served to thrust these political operations into the spotlight of postwar problems. An interest in the internal structure of Italy became a correlate of Allied concern with the external position of Italy in the whole Mediterranean picture.

This transition from limited military considerations to long-term policy considerations was neither natural nor easy for the American government. In order to make it, the United States had to reconcile differences between itself and the British government, and between itself and domestic public opinion. Furthermore, it had to do this outside the frame of reference provided by military necessity. Whatever was proposed for Italy had to be proposed on more debatable grounds than the conduct of the war.

Yet if it was difficult to formulate policy, it was impossible to avoid taking action on immediate questions. It is correct to read the Roosevelt-Churchill statement of September, 1944, as an effort to find a middle ground between the practical need to turn Italy into a going concern, the limitations imposed by a disturbed public opinion, and the implications of Soviet influence in southeastern Europe. At any rate, from the end of 1944 on, Italian political activities were scrutinized and approved or disapproved in relation to these points of reference. Thus, when the Department of State described the new Bonomi government of December, 1944, as ". . . supported by a majority of the political parties, comprising the Committee of National Liberation, and thus maintains a representative character," [4] the phrase must be understood to mean that a coalition had been arrived at in which competing political doctrines were so carefully balanced that none could give effective direction to more than the routine work of the Italian government.

That such were the actual limitations was clearly understood in Italy. It explains the efforts made by Italian political leaders to appeal to opinion in the United States over the head of the Control Commission by talking to journalists about anti-republicanism and British support of the monarchy. It also explains the failure of these efforts, for all finally had to face the trumps held by the Control Commission in the form of food, raw materials, and money. Even when political control was formally relaxed in February, 1945, there was little perceptible change. The only Italian government that could function was one that was able to secure a steady flow of economic and financial aid. This continued to mean a coalition in which conservative elements rested on a representative foundation of parties who disagreed with them on every essential point of internal policy, but who shared their estimate of the realities of the situation.

The final result was to draw a line between the Control Commission and the parties of the Left, especially the Communist party. An appreciation of the ease with which Togliatti, the Communist leader, could upset the fiction of a freely operating Italian government inevitably led the Control Commission to look on the Communist party as a dangerous and unpredictable element and to support the Christian Democrats by every means at its disposal.

The correct estimate that the Left-wing parties did not constitute a majority, and so did not have to be accepted as representing the will of the Italian people, did not alter the fact that they were in a strong position to force a crisis whose repercussions would run far beyond the borders of Italy. After 1944, the situation from week to week, based as it was on a complex interaction between Italian instability, the conduct of the war, and relations with Soviet Russia in neighboring areas, remained consistently delicate.

By this light it should not be difficult to understand the need that was felt to intervene in Italian affairs or the ultimate objectives at which Allied authority found itself aiming. With real power lodged in Allied hands it is a tribute not often enough paid to the fundamental good will of Anglo-American authority that this power was used with so high a degree of discretion. The only judgment that can be seriously made against this authority is that the responsibilities it assumed and the purposes it sought to achieve were not consistently pursued through the early stages of a postwar settlement.

It has been necessary to recount in some detail the situation that was presented to the American government as a result of its share in the combined control of the Mediterranean and of its part in the occupation and control of Italy. Even if many of the implications of these events reached the United States by reflection from the reactions of Great Britain, their impact cannot be doubted. Nor can it be ignored that they led to the rough definition of an American interest and to the hesitating development of an American policy. The growth of both interest and policy proceeded more rapidly and clearly through 1945 and 1946, and reached fruition in 1947; but the ground was prepared and the seeds planted in the climate of 1944.

The American position in the Mediterranean at the moment of pause, while the war against Germany was being concluded and the problem of building an all-out attack against Japan was absorbing the attention of Washington, can only be described as curious. A wide gap had developed between visible American power and the purposes for which it was being used. In the eyes of the American people and in the officially stated opinion of the American government, this power was being used to complete the defeat of Germany. To nations with traditional Mediterranean interests and to peoples living under the dispensation of a combined Anglo-American authority, the picture seemed different. In these eyes, American power was a present reality. If it supported no observable American interest, then it had to be assumed that it was tacitly serving the interests of Great Britain. It was locally impossible to believe that the United States was as indifferent to its strength as it professed to be. This judgment took a variety of forms, ranging from the communist view that the two capitalist powers naturally made common cause everywhere, to the Arab view that the United States was being drawn into sustaining British imperialism.

The American government was, however, officially unaware of the significance of its position. It made no effort to maintain it, even when it adopted courses of action that seemed to require its maintenance. Certainly there was no general appreciation in the United States of the extent to which the actual basis of power in the Mediterranean had shifted during the war from British to American shoulders. In consequence, the growing disparity between the British responsibility to maintain a Mediterranean system that would be serviceable to both Great Britain and America and the means available to carry out this responsibility passed unremarked except by a small number of interested observers.

As the war in Europe approached its conclusion, this disparity was revealed with an absoluteness that caught both American and British opinion off balance.

The British, in fact, had fallen into a policy of "as if," taking positions *as if* there had been no change in the distribution of power resources and *as if* American power in the Mediterranean was a demonstrably permanent factor. Such a course of action ultimately brought the United States face to face with the consequences of sharing a position of power and influence in the Mediterranean.

The immediate reaction was one of retreat. Public opinion rejected the thesis. Official opinion, regardless of courses already embarked on, repudiated the implication and called attention to tripartite unity and the general principles of the United Nations. This initial negative response did not develop, however, to the point where it interrupted the basic continuity of Anglo-American activities in the Mediterranean. Thus, while a policy of disassociation is to be noted, a practice of tacit collaboration must equally be remarked. The only conclusion that can be reached is that, on second thought, the American position was found to be so far developed and so essential to the international position of the United States that a decision to abandon it could not be taken.

This mixed response revealed the extent to which the public had lost touch with the actual movement of events. Opinion was clearly based on a set of stereotypes—anti-imperialist liberalism, democratic self-determination, co-operation with the Soviet Union—whose validity was being steadily lowered by circumstances. The most significant gap showed in connection with Soviet Russia.

Relations between the United States, Great Britain, and the Soviet Union had rested on mutual suspicion from 1920 to 1940. This attitude, surviving all official efforts to find a more workable ground, was modified in the months following the German attack on Russia. Public statements by Churchill and Roosevelt identified the Soviet Union as a victim of Nazi aggression and, by defining a common interest in resistance, laid the groundwork for the grand military alliance of 1942. The specified common interest was developed by every device of sustained publicity into a picture of a great and enduring ally sharing a common purpose. This creation was met more than halfway by those vague desires for social change and those unfulfilled hopes of a better world that twenty years of crises had generated in both the British and American peoples.

The vistas of international co-operation thus opened were not publicly tested during the tense uncertain stages of the war. General opinion settled into a pattern of conviction which said that an assumption of good faith was justified. The private experience of those who dealt with Soviet officials did not, however, confirm this public judgment. But experience accumulated slowly and did not work to modify the conviction that good faith was necessary to the conduct of the war and the only foundation for postwar co-operation.

Yet by the end of 1944 reservations began to show in the detailed application of this policy of confidence, and the possible contingency of it being unworkable was at least entertained. Discords of a kind that could not be ignored were heard. The tripartite agencies that had been set up at Teheran at the beginning of the year were not working satisfactorily. While it was not concluded that the Soviet Union was sabotaging the work, the suspicion grew that Russia was not interested in reaching hard and fast agreement about the future. This uneasiness was not communicated, however, beyond narrow official limits; and it was along this line that a gulf widened between official knowledge and public opinion.

The reasons for withholding this knowledge were many, and many of the reasons were good. Certainly there were strong arguments against disturbing existing strategic arrangements; and even the remote possibility of an international organization justified the maintenance of an open mind and silence.* The fact remains, however, that the gulf existed and, in late 1944, the shock produced on public feeling by events in the Mediterranean was wider than would have been the case if public and private information had been closer together. The combination of strong feeling and inexact knowledge made it easier to see these events as the product of British imperialism, or the revival of power politics, than to see them as rifts in tripartite unity.

* In connection with the vexed question of relations with Soviet Russia, only two points need to be insisted on: (a) that the so-called "tough" line was not acted upon until the assumption of good faith had been strained to the utmost, and (b) that, without assigning blame, Russian suspicions and policy hardened first and thus conditioned the hardening of American opinion.

VII. The Force of Circumstances: 1944

THE force of circumstances bore down the reservations and hesitations of the American government. This chapter is concerned with the pressure of these events. In the course of 1944 a very serious consideration came into play. A Mediterranean interest, widely felt to be compelling, developed without reference to the reluctances that have just been described. American and British interests in the oil reserves of the Middle East were joined into a common cause and gave rise to what was quickly assumed to be a common strategic interest.

Anglo-American conversations on the general subject of the world's petroleum resources began in Washington in April. The motivating forces behind these talks is obscure, but two chief purposes stand out. The U.S. Joint Chiefs of Staff were alarmed at the drain on continental American oil reserves and were eager, on long-range strategic grounds, to shift the burden of production to fields whose use would not directly affect American security. The Department of State, appreciating the tough competition that oil had previously introduced into international relations, was interested in raising the whole issue to the level of international agreement.*

* Other and less high-minded forces have been named as follows:

(a) Oil prospectors, thinly disguised as representatives of the Foreign Economic Administration, were reporting enthusiastically from the Middle East;

(b) American oil interests wanted to expand their rights while it was possible to bring pressure to bear on Great Britain and France;

At any rate, as the discussions proceeded, they led to an eminently reasonable statement of policy. It was recognized that "ample petroleum supplies . . . are necessary for the security and prosperity of nations; . . . [and] must be met by an orderly flow of oil from the various producing countries of the world." [1] Therefore, the two governments, hoping they would be supported by an enlightened public opinion, proposed to initiate a wider consultation with the United Nations that would lead to agreements carrying out the clause of the Atlantic Charter which provided for access on equal terms to the trade and raw material of the world. A combined Petroleum Council was set up to reduce these principles to practical working form.

The Soviet Union upset this atmosphere of good intentions in September, 1944, one month after the United States and Great Britain had reached a final agreement. It bluntly interjected a strategic and political note by demanding oil concessions in northern Iran. The Iranian government was unwilling to do anything that would serve to perpetuate Soviet influence in its northern provinces. The United States and Great Britain were equally unwilling that it should so act. They accordingly hesitated to press for favors in southern Iran which they knew would be refused to the Soviet Union in the north. They withdrew from the oil negotiations they had initiated. Tripartite relations in the area were plainly unequal to a strain of such magnitude. The Soviet Union, having expressed an interest and secured a reaction, rested its case for the time being.

The interposition of a Russian demand, while it did not alter the basic intentions of the British and American govern-

(c) The American-Arabian Oil Company had long been trying to draw the government in as a protecting agent for its venture in Saudi Arabia.

ments as far as the international control of petroleum resources was concerned, did clearly raise the specter of strategic interests and international competition. "Vital interests"
and "national security," in a context close to the heart of
oil-consuming military forces, entered the discussions and
were freely canvassed at military levels. Momentary concentration on petroleum brought the Middle East into focus as
an element in American security, and in turn linked it with
a larger complex of Mediterranean interests.*

As soon as oil appeared as a point of reference, other
problems of the Mediterranean fitted themselves into a more
easily understood pattern. Petroleum reserves in the Middle
East automatically raised the question of relations with the
Arab states. This in its turn raised questions of the position
of the French in the Levant and North Africa, of the disposition of Italy's colonies, and of the stability of Britain's
relations with the Arab world. Thus, these matters came to
American attention not as isolated issues, but as related
questions affecting a total American position. In this connection significant conversations were carried on, concurrently
with the petroleum talks, between the Department of State
and the British Foreign Office. Their purpose was to survey
the entire field of British and American aims in the Middle
East. From these conversations an informal understanding
emerged to the effect that, since these aims were not incompatible, the relations of both countries with the Arab world

* In so far as there was a tendency to find a strategic value in an
Anglo-American oil agreement, this hope was frustrated when the Agreement came to the Senate for ratification in January, 1945. American oil
companies lobbied so strenuously on the theme that the Agreement opened
the door for government interference and control that President Roosevelt
withdrew his request for approval.

The petroleum interest is discussed from another point of view on page
117 and following.

would be conducted co-operatively and with mutual frankness.

Against this complex background of war, strategic shifts, political implications, and the daily obligations imposed by the exercise of authority, the comparative influence as exercised in the Mediterranean by the United States and Great Britain became less determinable. So closely interlocked and interdependent were their attributes of power that it was increasingly difficult to draw a line between the interest of the one and the interests of the other. Only in the broad ranges of public opinion, or at high levels of policy, were differences preserved. In a growing number of cases this insistence bore little correspondence with working reality.

An immense combined military machine was in place, with administrative centers in Italy and Egypt. A related system of economic controls operated through the Allied Control Commission in Rome and the Middle East Supply Center in Cairo. Although the major obligation of these agencies was to support the war against Germany, their actual duties consisted, in great part, in administering Mediterranean affairs. American participation in all phases of their activities had steadily expanded as American resources became more and more essential to their successful continuance. The type and degree of direct American involvement varied widely from region to region.

But the result was that by the end of 1944 the United States was in a definable position in the Mediterranean. Responsibility had been accepted for the maintenance of considerable forces in the region, at least until the end of the war in Europe. Responsibility had been accepted for the rehabilitation of Italy. Responsibility had been accepted for the continued application of American power and influence, though not necessarily in military form, in the interest of effecting satisfactory postwar settlements.* The situation in the Mediterranean, however, did not permit a broadly generalized carrying out of these responsibilities. The Mediterranean presented concrete problems that required concrete answers. American action accordingly became increasingly positive within the Mediterranean frame of reference.

It is with this in mind that the Yalta Conference of February, 1945, is to be understood. From one point of view, Yalta can be described as an effort to chart the course of the future. It dealt with the defeat of Germany and it prepared for the entrance of Russia into the war against Japan. It created the machinery for future Great Power consultation. It reached preliminary agreements on a world security organization. But Yalta can equally be described as a Mediterranean Conference that failed. On its agenda appeared every discord of the preceding eight months, stated as specific issues. † A profound concern of the American and British

* These responsibilities were variously explained as:

(a) maintaining equilibrium pending the establishment of an international security organization;

(b) a policing activity to prevent prejudgment of a general peace settlement;

(c) a natural concomitant of the fact that the United States had a "vital interest" in a peaceful Europe;

(d) a process essential to making American influence felt on the international stage.

The worsening of American-Soviet relations in 1946 tended to emphasize the police and "vital interest" explanations, an emphasis that culminated in proposals to defend Greece and Turkey against totalitarian envelopment.

† These were: the composition of the Yugoslav government, the Italian-Yugoslav-Austrian frontier, Yugoslav-Bulgarian relations, Greek claims against Bulgaria, British and American financial claims and commercial rights in Rumania, the position of British and American representatives on the Allied Control Commissions in the Balkans, the unsatisfactory working of these Commissions, and, at the request of the Soviet Union, the status of the Straits.

See New York Times, March 25, 1947, for the full text of the Yalta Agreement, where the scope of the agenda was for the first time made known.

governments made itself clearly felt. This was to discover the intentions of the Soviet Union with respect to a series of points involving the Anglo-American position in the Mediterranean. Following that, it was to see if these problems could be compromised in the interest of tripartite relations. The nature of these problems was such that, unless they could be brought within the framework of a larger pattern of accord, they would remain as sources of future disagreement.

Seen from this aspect, Yalta ended the fiction of perfect compatibility between wartime allies by admitting that serious differences existed and by failing to resolve them. The specific issues of the Mediterranean region were not settled by piecemeal agreement, and the generalized agreement to which they were referred—the Declaration on Liberated Europe—rapidly proved both ambiguous and superficial. The consequent fact was that not only did the issues remain, but subsequent attention focused on their strategic implications. President Roosevelt's report to Congress on his return from Yalta contained an undertone of reservation.

> During the long period [between Teheran and Yalta], local problems were permitted to become acute in places like Poland and Greece and Italy and Yugoslavia. . . .
>
> There have been instances of political confusion and unrest. . . . Worse than that, there actually began to grow up . . . vaguely defined ideas of "spheres of influence" which were incompatible with the basic principles of international collaboration. . . .
>
> The three most powerful nations have agreed . . . to help the people of any liberated area, or of any former satellite state, to solve their own . . . problems through formally established democratic processes. . . .
>
> We shall not always have ideal solutions. . . . [2]

This unresolved discussion of Mediterranean power relations had another important consequence. It made the
Mediterranean a frankly recognized component of tripartite
relations on the continent of Europe. In the long run, those
relations—say in Germany or Austria—could not be any
better than they were in the Balkans, the Middle East, or
Italy. And, conversely, the Mediterranean reverted to its
former status of being "a string which, when pulled, revealed
that its other end was in India, Vladivostok, the Middle
Danube, or Mosul." It is symbolical that the year which
began with Yalta ended with the courtesy visit of the *U.S.S.*
Providence to Athens.

In the months following the Yalta Conference, the United
States extended its explicit policy beyond the international
commitments it had accepted under the Atlantic Charter and
the Declaration of the United Nations. The first extension
was a statement of the thesis that a re-establishment of
economic and social stability in Europe was essential to the
making and maintenance of peace. The second was a firm
statement that a satisfactory peace settlement required the
prevention of territorial change by unilateral action. These
extensions represented an unusual degree of official commitment because their application required a willingness to take
positive action.

The establishment of economic and social stability meant—
if it was to mean anything—indirect intervention in the
internal affairs of other nations. The prevention of territorial
change had to envisage the possible use of force. And these
extensions of policy took on particular significance when they
were defined as protecting the security of the United States.
The Department of State, in reply to a communication from
members of Congress, said:

President Roosevelt pursued a firm foreign policy whereby the United States participated as an active force in all foreign questions involving American interests . . . used his influence and that of the United States as [a] mediator in those questions which, although not directly affecting our interests, might disturb international harmony. . . . [Yet] characterizing President Roosevelt as playing primarily a mediator role in European areas is doing an injustice . . . since he pursued in those areas a policy looking towards the concrete objectives for which we fought, rather than a policy of the disinterested mediator.[3]

The Yalta Agreement was of little practical use to Anglo-American authorities in the Mediterranean. It solved none of the pressing issues in which they were interested. Every item of immediate concern had merely been noted for future consideration. But, on the other hand, nothing had been said that called for a change in the courses of action already being followed. Policy in Italy and Greece conformed with the general principles of the Declaration on Liberated Europe. The steps that had been taken in those countries to maintain economic and social stability were, therefore, presumably approved. And, finally, although a pattern for tripartite collaboration on a world scale had been sketched, Anglo-American collaboration on the Mediterranean scale had not been disapproved.

VIII. Acceptance of the Inevitable: 1945

DURING the rest of 1945 the Anglo-American position was subjected to considerable testing. The pressure was felt also on American policy. That the effect of this pressure was to fix the outlines of that policy is a thing more easily gauged by its present form than by the evidence of any single step in the process. The first test came in Venezia Giulia.

The desire of Yugoslavia to anticipate a peace settlement by occupying Trieste and its hinterland had been foreseen by Allied Force Headquarters in Italy. Tito's antagonistic policy, following liberation, was a sufficient warning. The Anglo-American Command in February, 1945, negotiated an agreement defining the line on which Allied and Yugoslav forces would meet and stand when the Germans surrendered.[1] The moment, however, was awaited warily.

When it arrived, a New Zealand contingent was rushed through the collapsing German army and occupied Trieste on May 2, the day on which Kesselring's surrender was announced. Simultaneously, the Yugoslav partisans fanned out through Istria, Carinthia, and Styria. Tito immediately claimed a right of conquest. The Yugoslav Press Agency in London stated that "the Allies have entered Trieste without our permission. This might have undesirable consequences." During the following week American troops moved into Trieste, the Yugoslavs took control of the civil administration of Venezia Giulia, the issue entered Italian politics, and the Department of State released an account of the situation to the American public, resting its position on the need to prevent a unilateral settlement of a territorial claim.

The incident posed a variety of problems and clearly showed how interlocking Mediterranean issues had become. Aside from its prejudicial effect on ultimate international agreement, it raised the question of Italian-Yugoslav relations at an inconveniently early date. Furthermore, the maintenance of the territorial *status quo* was tied up with strategic considerations, for behind Yugoslavian insistence was presumably a Soviet interest in pushing into the Mediterranean.

Tito, when his agreement of February was referred to, explained that the problem was no longer military; it had become political. At this point the Anglo-American Command transferred the issue to the British and American governments. On May 14 the two governments sent similar notes to Tito, asserting that the debated Italian provinces must remain under Allied Military Government pending a peace conference and calling on him to withdraw his troops.

The Yugoslav government made no reply. Its local representatives continued to prejudge the future to the utmost of their power. A Trieste "Assembly" was convened. A local propaganda machine was set to work.* The next step was left to Allied Force Headquarters. Although the issue had been moved from the military to the political level, it still contained an important military element. If the Yugoslavs had to be shifted by force, what force was available, and if the force were applied, to what extent could Tito count on the support of the Soviet Union?

* *Nostro Avvenire*, an Italian-language paper in Trieste, raised an ideological-strategic issue: "Trieste is a bastion, which once wrenched from reactionary imperialism, has attained an advanced position in a new and truly democratic world."—Quoted in the New York *Times*, March 18, 1945.

No real intelligence on this point was obtainable and the force available to the Allied Command was limited. Faced with these facts British judgment showed a wish to temporize, arguing that the matter should be treated as a local frontier controversy and compromised at the lowest level compatible with strategic needs. The United States, however, stood on principle, arguing first that a failure to force Tito's withdrawal would release a flood of similar incidents and vitiate all hope of a broad peaceful settlement in Europe, and secondly that Tito had gone beyond his Soviet support and would back down. In proof of these convictions it was willing to commit American personnel to any eventuality.

The American view prevailed. Allied troops were prepared for an operation. This preparation included a public statement from Field Marshal Alexander, as Supreme Allied Commander, explaining the situation.* This statement served also as an unofficial ultimatum to Tito and obviated further exchange. On May 21 the Yugoslav forces began to evacuate, and on May 22 Tito accepted the Anglo-American position "in principle." The incident was considered closed by the drawing of the Morgan Line.

As far as the American government was concerned, it had defined its position in the words, "It is the firm policy of the United States, as its Allies have been officially informed, that territorial changes should be made only after thorough study and after full consultation and deliberation between the

* ". . . Marshal Tito's apparent intention to establish his claims by force of arms . . . [is] all too reminiscent of Hitler, Mussolini and Japan. It is to prevent such actions that we have been fighting this war. . . . We cannot now throw away vital principles for which we have all fought. Under these principles it is our duty to hold these disputed territories as trustees. . . ."
Full text, New York *Times*, May 20, 1945.

various governments concerned . . . in order not to preju-
dice, through sudden unilateral action taken in the flush of
victory, a final solution corresponding to the problems and
the principles involved." [2] It must be noted, however, that
this principle had been impaired in advance at Yalta in the
case of Poland, and that in the instances where it could be
effectively applied, there existed a solid foundation of available force. The principle was immediately open to widely
differing interpretations. Its meaning, as enunciated in Washington, bore little resemblance to its meaning as understood
by those whom it restrained. To the latter, it was plainly a
device for perpetuating any desired *status quo*.

In the particular instance of Venezia Giulia, the conclusion
was drawn that the United States had defined an interest in
the Mediterranean. It was further assumed that this interest
was closely related to British strategic interests and that the
factor which had conditioned this definition was the Soviet
Union. The implications of this view were clearly appreciated
by Anglo-American agencies in the Mediterranean. Their
estimates of its significance were rapidly communicated to
higher governmental levels. The opinion of the American
government underwent an important change.

There was no further question of basic differences between
the American and British governments with respect to Italy:
both now agreed on the fundamental purpose for which Italy
was being revived. A common line was found with respect
to Greece; and although the official responsibility remained
British, it was given consistent American support. Elsewhere
in the Mediterranean, east and west, an Anglo-American
position was allowed to become more explicit.

The Mediterranean scene generally offered, in 1945, a
rich variety of situations that called for Anglo-American

collaboration. In the course of eight months every possible source of trouble, from Azerbaijan to the Pillars of Hercules, became active. At each point a traditional British interest met an intangible Soviet pressure. The United States, with an already heavy investment of international principles and local commitments but without a defined and comprehensive policy for the Mediterranean, discovered unexpected interests on every hand and grew familiar with the interlocking nature of even the simplest issues. The British government assumed, somewhat too hopefully at times, that a general identity of interest between itself and the United States was inevitable. Soviet opinion on this point was not expressed until a later date, but then it was made clear that it too had assumed an identity. The American government, though it continued officially to repudiate a common interest, at least admitted to running a parallel course with Great Britain.

In May, 1945, the French government once again sought to retain ground in the Levant. Conventional troubles broke out in conventional forms. The situation did not, however, develop conventionally, for Syria and Lebanon had been recognized as independent nations by the United States and Great Britain, and their governments were hypersensitive to pressure from France. In addition, the first steps in the formation of an Arab League had been taken in February, with marked British approval, and the Arab world was more than eager to put in a claim to defend its compatriots. The British government, which a short time before had seen no reason why France should not have a position in the Levant comparable to that of Great Britain in Iraq, sharply changed its mind. Its position in the Middle East now plainly required that the French withdraw from an area where Arab dislike of their methods might easily be converted into antagonism against Western Europe as a whole.

The French, in the guise of deploying troops to the Far East, sent the cruiser *Jeanne d'Arc*, loaded as a transport, to the scene. The British and American governments co-ordinated their handling of the issue. The United States informed France that:

> An impression has been created . . . that French representatives have been using the threat of force to obtain from Syria and Lebanon concessions of a political, cultural, and military nature. . . .
>
> It is important [that], at the very time when the International Security Organization is in process of being created . . . all nations . . . refrain from any act which might give rise to a suspicion . . . that a member of the future organization may be pursuing a policy not in conformity with the spirit and principles which that organization is being established to defend.[3]

Concurrently, the British government stated that its troops in Syria would intervene to restore order and requested the French to return their troops to barracks to avoid incidents. It was further suggested that a conference be called to dispose of the issue. This ultimatum, with face-saving delays, was accepted.

Then the Soviet Union, which had been silent up to this point, informed all the great powers that it viewed the situation with alarm and insisted that "speedy measures to stop military operations in Syria and Lebanon must be taken, and the conflict which had arisen must be settled in a peaceful manner." This sudden interest was not taken at its face value. France welcomed it as a balancing force and sought to escape from the nutcracker of a limited conference with the United

States and Great Britain by proposing to include the Soviet
Union in a conference at which all the unresolved problems
of the Middle East would be canvassed. The United States
and Great Britain were in complete agreement that they had
no wish at that time to be dragged into controversies with
other powers about the future of the Middle East. The
proposal was disregarded.

A relatively peaceful impasse was arrived at. British troops
were in effective control. The Arab League passed vitriolic
resolutions. The French government made a wild and fruit-
less effort to refer the issue to the still unorganized United
Nations. But, in effect, the situation settled down. Three
significant features of the dispute are to be remarked: the
evident decision to exclude France from the eastern Mediterranean in the interest of preserving good relations with
the Arab world; the appearance of the Soviet Union; and
the complete correlation of American and British policy and
action.

Meanwhile a smaller problem arose at the other end of
the Mediterranean. The Spanish government, stimulated by
hints that the time was come to look into its illegal occupation of the Tangier International Zone, indicated that it
would welcome a study and regularization of the situation.
The British and French governments, the important surviving signatories of the Statute of 1928, invited the United
States to take part in informal conversations. The preliminary
soundings, however, revealed a lack of unanimity. France,
seeing an opportunity to restore her prestige in North
Africa and Morocco, wanted her previous preponderance of
influence to be restored, and, to make this point entirely
clear, was not only ready but anxious to have the Spaniards
ostentatiously driven out by French Moroccan troops. The

United States and Great Britain privately agreed that a French adventure could not be permitted. Publicly, they proposed to include Spanish representatives in the conference.

A date was set for a meeting in Paris, and military, naval, economic, and political opinions were assembled. At this stage the Soviet Union asked to be included, stating that she was automatically interested in all international conferences. However, the Soviet Union saw no reason for respecting a Spanish interest and categorically refused to enter into discussions with a fascist state. This request caused considerable confusion. To avoid an issue being made, a temporary solution, in which the Soviet Union quietly concurred, was quickly and informally agreed without conference. The *status quo ante* was to be restored pending the calling of a conference at some suitable later date. Spain withdrew her troops and Tangier reverted to its old-fashioned international form.* Except for the irruption of a Soviet interest, the Tangier story was unimportant; but this one aspect was noted as an additional item in Anglo-American experience.

Greece was a more significant scene of trouble. The civil war had settled nothing. The country continued to be disputed between Greek Communists and anti-Communists, and between the Greek government and the Slavic governments of the Balkans. In addition, it became an issue between Great Britain and the Soviet Union at the international level. The British government maintained a precarious stability in the

---

* The re-establishment of international control was enlivened by two events. The French stole a march on their colleagues by sending a cruiser from Casablanca with military units and press photographers aboard. Their part in the ceremony was accordingly played with appropriate pomp and publicity and gave the Spanish withdrawal something of the appearance of a retreat. In addition, a rumor was circulated that Soviet representatives were coming to join the reconstructed international authority. This provided an agitating but unsatisfied stir.

face of the declining authority of the Greek government and the increasing impoverishment and physical ruin of the Greek people. The groundwork for permanent improvement could not be laid. Policy, on the part of the Greek government, wavered between impotent suppression and grasping for outside aid. Pressure on the Greek frontier from Yugoslavia, Bulgaria, and Albania was unremitting. As a constant reminder of greater issues, Soviet propaganda talked of "reactionary imperialism," and the Greek Communists asserted that Tito's soldiers—five hundred thousand of them—were ready to help the Greek people against the British.

Great Britain, in the unenviable position of being obliged to support any Greek government in order to prevent the alternative of a national collapse, was led into being held responsible for the actions of those governments. It was accurate but useless for Prime Minister Kanellopoulos to insist that there was only one problem to be solved: the restoration of social stability on a broad but simple basis of food, clothing, and personal security. This was the essential preliminary to economic and political rehabilitation. Until this was done the government moved in a vicious circle: instability among the masses created a favorable field for communism; the spread of communism increased the diehard tendencies of the political Right; heightened political tension lowered confidence and made economic revival impossible; and delay in reorganizing the national economy increased the instability of the masses.[4] But there was no breathing space in which to develop the means to check the swing around such a circle.

Yet Great Britain could not let go. Withdrawal could only mean that civil strife would flare up; and civil war could only end, barring outside intervention, with the expansion of Communist authority and, hence, of Soviet influence into the Greek peninsula. The strategic consequences of this were not acceptable.

Throughout the whole of this difficult period the United States supported Great Britain, refraining from criticism and standing firmly by the British position on all occasions. Inside Greece there was full co-operation between the two embassies. Even the United States Information Service, so pointedly disassociated the year before, now co-ordinated its work with that of its neighbor. The American press quieted down to a normal murmur of doctrinaire discontent. By the end of the year the two governments stood on so common a ground that their actions and reactions in the area were calculably complementary.

The speed with which this relationship developed was a direct consequence of events in the Balkans. The growth of a uniform attitude toward Yugoslavia has been described. A similar growth took place with respect to the former satellites, Rumania and Bulgaria. Starting afresh from the Yalta Agreement, the situation in these two states continued, in the American and British view, to grow steadily worse. This deterioration, which implied an equivalent deterioration in tripartite relations in the area, was reported to the public, but not in a form that made it easy to relate it with problems in Greece or to general Anglo-American interests in the Mediterranean. That correlation was, however, a commonplace procedure for the Anglo-American agencies in the region. There it was concluded that the basic Yalta Declaration on Liberated Europe was not being honored, and that the interim governments of the Balkan satellites, far from preparing the ground for the establishment of representative institutions, were being dominated by their Communist members to the advantage of the Soviet Union.

There is not space to follow in detail the steps by which official American opinion moved from doubts about Soviet intentions in southeastern Europe to a conviction that those intentions were dangerous. Reports from the area, however, built up the following general picture. The local Communist parties in each country used propaganda, economic pressure, and terrorism to confuse and intimidate the electorate. The Communist members of coalition governments disorganized the opposition parties and discredited their leaders by tactics of delay, frustration, and threats. The Soviet Union, by its interpretation of the armistice terms, was deliberately breaking down the economic order of these states and transferring the control of key activities to Russian hands. The Soviet Union was setting up indoctrinated military units, composed of returned Rumanian and Bulgarian prisoners of war. The Soviet representatives on the Allied Control Commissions worked closely with local Communists and intervened in their favor in the decisions of the coalition governments. The Allied Control Commissions were so completely dominated by the Soviet Union that their British and American members could not prevent these developments. To round off everything, the atmosphere in which the British and American Delegations lived and worked was so fantastic a mixture of Balkan espionage, of petty restrictions imposed by Russian design and suspicion, and of a lack of adequate and timely guidance from Washington and London that only the hardiest extroverts could maintain the proper degree of detachment and balance.

Since this picture implied the slow, steady, and sure expansion and consolidation of Soviet influence and authority, its effect was to emphasize the contradictory elements in American policy. The intention to explore every possibility of three-power agreement was weakened by actual experience of three-power disagreement at the point of closest contact. Equally important, however, was the fact that an effective response to these situations was inhibited by the will to continue the search for agreement on the larger scale. The inevitable result of this implicit contradiction was the development of two schools of official thought. It became apparent, in the closing months of 1945, that many elements of the American government were prepared to shift ground with respect to the Soviet Union, but that they lacked the means to conduct a successful debate with those who were not so prepared. The unsettled state of official opinion, by making it difficult to give clear guidance to representatives abroad, opened the way to *ad hoc* decisions for which there was a considerable undercurrent of sympathy.

Thus the Mediterranean tended to become an area in which an alternative to the policy of tripartite accord first appeared as a possibility. This alternative, which can be roughly described as one of preventing the Soviet Union from establishing positions within the Mediterranean basin, was supported by many strategic, economic, and political considerations. In fact it was almost impossible to carry out the responsibilities that had been assumed in Italy or to protect the interests that had developed in the Middle East without partially accepting this alternative as valid.

In any event, this course, even if not explicitly adopted, was not explicitly checked. A curious situation resulted in which the British and American governments, while insisting on their freedom of diplomatic action, looked to their Combined Command in the Mediterranean to implement that action. It is difficult to see how the co-ordination of American and British interests could have been prevented in these circumstances; and it is easy to see why a sense of jointly resisting Soviet pressure developed. Certainly the Soviet Union acted to confirm this feeling.

In November, 1945, the United States proposed that the terms of the tripartite agreement with Iran be anticipated and that the Three Powers withdraw their troops immediately. The Soviet Union rejected this proposal. A month later the Iran Workers Party revolted against the government in Teheran. In December the Soviet Union expressed a desire to establish bases in the Dodecanese Islands off the Mediterranean coast of Turkey. At the same time a propaganda campaign was started in which historic Russian rights in the Turkish provinces of Kars and Ardahan were elaborately developed.*

There were common factors in all of the situations that have been described in this chapter. The Soviet Union appeared as an interested party in each case. Each raised the question of the possible extension of Soviet influence into the Mediterranean region. Though widely separated geographically, each was of direct consequence either to the British or to the Anglo-American position in the Mediterranean. Finally, the American and the British reactions to these situations were co-ordinated and consistent.

The regular recurrence of these factors led, by the end

* An additional irritant came when the Soviet Union presented a claim of $300,000,000 for reparations against Italy. At the UNRRA Council in London in September, 1945, the United States asked for and pushed through a proposal to make UNRRA operations in Italy full scale—as in Greece and Yugoslavia—and to raise the allotment from $150,000,000 to $450,000,000. The Soviet Union and its adherents resisted vigorously but were overridden. Three months later this hitherto unmentioned reparation claim was put forward.

of the year, to a loosely consolidated Anglo-American front in the Mediterranean. Its stated purpose was to maintain the stability of that region until an international security organization was effectively established. Its activities, however, seemed to take the form of preserving a conventional *status quo* and of defending established interests. An observer needed only to move from one power position to another to see the reasonableness of either interpretation. Such a front, since it did not reflect an equal degree of Anglo-American co-ordination in other aspects of policy than those directly concerned with the Mediterranean, was subject to unexpected modification. For the moment, however, and in the given context, it was a fact.

IX. Mediterranean Peace Conference: 1946

THROUGHOUT 1946, under the surface of events, the course of American action in the Mediterranean became settled. The increasing success with which the Communist parties consolidated their control of the Balkan satellites worked to stiffen British policy in Greece, and American relations with Yugoslavia narrowed still further the aims of Anglo-American policy in Italy. Perceptibly, throughout the Mediterranean, fragmented nationalisms were being re-grouped under the compelling influence of larger interests. The Balkans, Allied and satellite alike, were, with the exception of Greece, orienting themselves toward the Soviet Union and finding a ground for unity in a combination of Slavic sentiment and Communist ideology. Less directly, Great Britain was encouraging an equivalent co-ordination of the Arab states.*

It was clear that, in the eastern Mediterranean and its hinterland, the surfaces of opposing interests had come tightly together and that the least movement in one directly grated on the other. There was no "buffer area," no toler-ated vacuum to soften their contacts. So precarious did the balance between them seem that it could be plausibly argued that, if the Anglo-American position were abandoned at any

* The first meeting of these states, called at British persuasion at Alexandria in 1944, had produced nothing. In February, 1945, however, a second conference at Cairo led rapidly to the formation of the Arab League, consisting of Egypt, Saudi Arabia, Yemen, Iraq, Trans-Jordan, Syria, and Lebanon.

one point, the entire position would be undermined. On the Soviet side it could be argued with equal plausibility that the pressures being exerted could not be withdrawn or reduced without endangering the extended position that the Soviet Union had reached in Europe in consequence of victory. A change on either side of the balance might conceivably lead to profound modifications in the structure of the international power system not in Europe alone, but throughout the world. The friction generated by such a situation heated every issue and inevitably carried over into the conferences that met to consider peace treaties for Italy and the satellite states.

It is not necessary to survey in detail the events of this year in the Mediterranean. Their cumulative effect is their most important feature.* It is enough to point out that they

---

* A chronological list is given, however, for reference.
(a) *January*
   (1) U.S.S.R. brings question of British in Greece to U.N.
   (2) Britain extends loan of £10,000,000 to Greece.
   (3) U.N. takes up question of U.S.S.R. troops in Iran.
(b) *February*
   (1) Syria protests British and French troops to U.N.
   (2) Yugoslavia protests Polish troops in Italy to U.N.
   (3) U.S. loans $10,000,000 to Greece.
(c) *March*
   (1) Conflict between U.S.S.R. and Iran in the province of Azerbaijan.
   (2) U.N. takes up question of Franco regime in Spain.
   (3) Great Britain and Egypt open question of 1936 Treaty.
   (4) Tito negotiates pacts with Poland and Czechoslovakia.
   (5) Greek elections—anti-Communist victory.
(d) *April*
   (1) U.S.S.R. and Iran sign oil agreement.
   (2) *U.S.S. Missouri* visits Athens and Istanbul.
   (3) Foreign Ministers begin study of peace treaties at Paris.
(e) *May*
   (1) U.S.S.R. and Iran again come before U.N.
   (2) Foreign Ministers reach and stall over Trieste.
   (3) Albania fires on British naval ships.
   (4) Arab leaders confer in Cairo on Palestine and the Egyptian Treaty. [Footnote continued on page 78.]

provided a constant preoccupation in the conferences of the Foreign Ministers, the Security Council and Assembly of the United Nations, and the Peace Conference at Paris. Although on each of these occasions the material was re-studied and the issues were re-examined, no solutions were found that in any way broke the stalemate that had developed in the Mediterranean.

The meetings of the Foreign Ministers and their Deputies in London (September, 1945), in Moscow (December, 1945), in Paris (April-July, 1946), and the Peace Conference in Paris (July-October, 1946)—both by what they did and what they were unable to do—revealed the basic undercurrents that were at work. The draft treaties, completed by the Foreign Ministers and referred to the Peace Conference, contained two groups of unagreed clauses: one involving economic issues, the other strategic issues. Both, however, were directly connected with the facts of power relations in the Mediterranean.*

The lines thus drawn carried over to the full Peace Conference. There Mr. Molotov, speaking on the economic clauses of the satellite treaties, insisted that the Soviet Union would oppose all outside interference in the economic life of those states. Only in this way could democratic institutions be consolidated and the revival of fascism be prevented. Mr. Byrnes replied that the United States insisted on the

(f) *June*
    (1) Britain and U.S. announce revised armistice terms for Italy.
    (2) Italy votes to establish a republic.

* Mr. Byrnes records: "One of the things that gave us particular concern . . . was the unmistakable evidence of Russian expansion. . . . Her determination to dominate the Balkan states had become apparent, . . . [she] had made a bid for control of one of Italy's North African colonies; . . . [we were] convinced that the Soviets' interest . . . was primarily military." James F. Byrnes, *Speaking Frankly*, Harper, 1947, p. 92.

Open Door because that was the only way to prevent the establishment of an economic system which would "merely substitute for Germany some other country upon which they [the satellite states] would be almost entirely dependent for supplies and markets."[1] With the oppositions clearly stated, the debate proceeded through an immense irrelevancy of detailed claims. Finally a standard clause was written into all the treaties granting equality of treatment in commercial matters to all of the United Nations for a period of eighteen months from ratification. This compromised the appearance but not the substance of the issue. Debate on the free use of the Danube followed the same course, used the same arguments, and came to the same end.

On the purely strategic side, Trieste was the key issue. The Foreign Ministers had rung all possible changes on the subject and reluctantly accepted the idea of a free territory.* In the full Conference, however, Yugoslavia attacked this agreement. The United States and Great Britain opposed any modification. Mr. Molotov welcomed a fresh approach; he was convinced that, since Italy's claims could not be conscientiously defended, the United States was chiefly concerned to ensure the continuance of Anglo-American control. The United States stood firm in the face of violent lobbying and of proposals to reduce the Italian navy and to admit the Balkan states as coadministrators, and remained undisturbed when Yugoslavia withdrew from the Conference. At the end, the original agreement was accepted, but

* At a private meeting between Mr. Byrnes and Mr. Molotov, the latter had suggested his willingness to alter his stand on Italian reparations and colonies if all of Venezia Giulia including Trieste were ceded to Yugoslavia. The rejection of this proposition led Mr. Vishinsky, who was also present, to a prolonged remark on American "imperialist expansion."

See Byrnes, op. cit., p. 128.

it was recognized as a superficial compromise in that it did no more than temporarily neutralize an issue that could not be resolved. The most that even Mr. Byrnes could say for it was that "Italy has been disarmed so that aggressive action cannot be supported, and Yugoslavia, despite its militant nationalism, will hesitate, I believe, to challenge the authority of the Security Council in this area." [2]

The Conference at last returned amended drafts to the Foreign Ministers for their final agreement. All of the Great Powers professed themselves discontented with the result. The Soviet Union stated that the United States and Great Britain had shown themselves more concerned to defend and expand the interests of "capitalist imperialism" than to achieve "a truly democratic and peaceful world." The United States left its journalists to express the feeling that the Soviet Union was more interested in keeping the Red Army in Europe than in reaching agreement on outstanding issues. At one point, during the final session of the Foreign Ministers in New York (November, 1946), Mr. Byrnes let it be known that he felt that "The demands made by Mr. Molotov for the conclusion of [the] treaties, . . . made continuation of the *status quo* the more attractive alternative." [3]

Yet, measured by strengthened or weakened influence, the results were not wholly unsatisfactory to the Soviet Union. Its position in southeastern Europe was unshaken, but Anglo-American influence in Italy had been partially compromised. The Anglo-American position in the Mediterranean was intact, but its intangible foundations in human loyalties were less firm. Soviet protégés had been given an ideological field day and become more politically cohesive; but Small Power opinion, on which both the United States and Great Britain relied, was still diversified and suspicious.

As far as the Mediterranean region was concerned, the results of the Peace Conference made adjustments in both policy and method inevitable. For the United States, the line was that which Mr. Byrnes had laid down in February:

> Though the *status quo* is not sacred and unchangeable, we cannot overlook a unilateral gnawing away at [it] . . . we cannot allow aggression to be accomplished by coercion or pressure or by subterfuges such as political infiltration. . . . We must make it clear in advance that we intend to act to prevent aggression, making it clear at the same time that we will not use force for any other purpose. . . . I am convinced that satisfactory solutions can be found if there is a stop to this maneuvering for strategic advantage all over the world. . . .[4]

As this guidance was turned into action in the Mediterranean, the position of power which the United States had so casually acquired during the war came unmistakably to be used as a support for policy in 1946. The adjustment of American aims to this reading of Soviet intentions obviously called for the firm retention of all the positions from which power and influence could be made felt. Of such positions throughout the world, the Anglo-American position in the Mediterranean was an important one, and it was correspondingly supported. The mounting scale of loans to Greece and Italy, the decisive hardening of attitude toward all issues, a rising concern with the shifting political tensions of the region—all are evidence of the place that the Mediterranean had come to occupy in American thinking.

The Soviet Union, for its part, made its adjustments by increasing the variety and extent of its pressures on the circumference of the Mediterranean basin. It supplemented them with propaganda designed to encourage every disintegrating force that could be found or developed within the region; and from the international platform of the United Nations, it consistently sought to stimulate those groups of opinion that might make difficult or inhibit the effective exercise of Anglo-American authority.*

The Mediterranean region was accordingly marked out as an area in which opposing purposes and interests came into recognized conflict. The build-up of American power and its partial co-ordination with historical British positions was one factor in the definition of this conflict. The other, equally significant and compelling, was the fixing of Russian land power far to the west in Europe and the penetration

* A second chronological list is given for reference.
(a) *July*
  (1) Communist-organized strike in Anglo-Iranian Oil Company.
  (2) Peace Conference opens in Paris.
(b) *August*
  (1) U.S.S.R. proposes joint control of Straits with Turkey.
  (2) Yugoslavia shoots down U.S. planes.
(c) *September*
  (1) Guerrilla warfare reopens in Macedonia.
  (2) Palestine Conference in London.
  (3) U.S. protests preparations for Bulgarian elections, which are held and strengthen Communist position.
  (4) King George of Greece reaches Athens.
(d) *October*
  (1) U.S. loans $25,000,000 to Greece.
  (2) U.S. reimburses Italy $50,000,000.
  (3) Albania mines British naval ships.
  (4) U.S. protests preparations for Rumanian elections, which are held and strengthen Communist position.
(e) *November*
  (1) Anglo-American financial experts confer on Greece.
(f) *December*
  (1) Greece protests Yugoslav aid to guerrillas to U.N.
  (2) U.S. reimburses Italy $51,000,000.
  (3) Standard-Socony Oil Companies reach agreement with Anglo-Iranian Oil Company.
(g) *January, 1947*
  (1) U.S. Loan to Italy $100,000,000.
  (2) British Parliamentary report on Greece.

of Soviet influence and interest—by way of Yugoslavia—to the Adriatic Sea. Leaving on one side related economic and political questions, the balance of force in Europe was dangerously fluid. Two external influences, the Soviet Union and the United States, had simultaneously appeared. The projection of the one by land overlapped and was overlapped by the sea and air projection of the other. The point of highest tension in this overlap inevitably developed in the area where American sea and air power could be made most easily effective against vulnerable parts of the Soviet Union.*

It was not surprising, therefore, that the Soviet Union made its most open effort at adjustment in connection with Turkey and the control of the Straits, nor that the United States and Great Britain were quick, decisive, and of one opinion in their counteractions. The Soviet Union had long served notice of its interest in revising the Montreux Convention. At Yalta, and again at Potsdam, it had put this item on the agenda. On both occasions Great Britain and the United States kept the door open for consultation at a later date; and, at Potsdam, had specifically agreed that "the Convention . . . should be revised as failing to meet present-day conditions," and that "as the next step the matter should be the subject of direct conversations between each

---

* Walter Lippmann put the situation with precision. "The Russians' preoccupation now is not how to keep the Dardanelles open but how to close them . . . to the Anglo-Americans. . . . The Russian view is . . . that unless they control Turkey . . . Britain and America will, in case of war, not only use the Dardanelles to enter the Black Sea with their enormously preponderant fleets but they will use the northern coasts of Turkey . . . as a base for aerial and amphibian attacks. . . ."—New York *Herald Tribune*, September 5, 1946.

"The Red Army, which dominates eastern Europe, and could not be removed by a diplomatic frontal attack, can be outflanked in the eastern Mediterranean."—New York *Herald Tribune*, November 2, 1946.

of the three Governments and the Turkish Government." [5]

In November, 1945, the United States, in accordance with this procedure, sent a note to Turkey proposing a conference. Great Britain, though feeling no urgency to raise the question, approved in principle. The Soviet Union took no action. Almost a year later, however, it sent the Turkish government its own set of proposals. They aimed at settling the problem by excluding America and Britain. They asserted that the control of the Straits concerned the Black Sea powers alone, and stated that Turkey and Russia, "as the Powers most interested and capable," should consult on the establishment of joint means of defense.

The background for this abrupt suggestion was not of a kind to persuade the Turkish government that its acceptance would be in the best interest of the nation. The denunciation of the Soviet-Turkish Treaty a year before had been followed by a pointed propaganda campaign and by rumored troop movements in the Balkans and the Caucasus, which had kept the Turkish army in a state of constant and expensive mobilization. The Turkish government reported the proposals to the United States and Great Britain, explaining that they had included the setting up of Soviet bases on Turkish soil. These two governments promptly informed the Soviet Union that the Straits were an international concern and that the phrase "direct conversations" did not mean attempting to reach a unilateral settlement. The United States added that "in its opinion the Government of Turkey should continue to be primarily responsible for the defense of the Straits and that should the Straits become the object of attack or threat of attack by an aggressor, the resulting situation would be a matter for action on the part of the Security Council of the United Nations." [6]

Thus guided and supported, the Turkish government rejected the Soviet proposals. The Soviet Union repeated its contention. America and Britain repeated their contention. Turkey rejected the second note. The Soviet Union took no further action. In fact, no further action was possible short of the use of force. The significant features of this exchange were the frankness with which Russia stated the basic strategic interest involved, and the promptness with which the United States accepted the issue as a test case. Acting Secretary of State Acheson, in reply to a press question on the subject, said that he supposed his questioner was wondering why the United States now took an interest, when it had not been sufficiently concerned at an earlier date even to sign the Montreux Convention. That it had not been interested was, he thought, a reflection on American foreign policy. At the same time the Secretary of the Navy announced that naval forces were being maintained in the Mediterranean for two purposes—to support the Allied Military Governments and to protect United States interests and support United States policy in the area.[7]

The issue is still unresolved. In spite of an official willingness to carry it to the level of international discussion, it does not seem likely that this will be done in the near future. The American decision in March, 1947, to strengthen the military effectiveness of Turkey had some of the tone of an informal ultimatum and probably pinned the question at the strategic level for some time to come.

X. The Truman Doctrine: 1947

THE United States had traveled a long way in the Mediterranean from 1942 to have reached a point at which it could speak clearly of interests and policy. Without attempting an immediate description of these interests, it can be said that they rested on a strange and only half-understood foundation. They did not rest upon an American position. They depended upon the continuation of an Anglo-American position. The United States acting alone could support them only by a considerable redistribution of its military force and by an extensive reorientation of its diplomatic agencies. American power could not in this region be immediately separated from a British system of authority and influence.

The practical implications of this relationship were revealed at the end of 1946 and the start of 1947. Basic weaknesses began to show in Great Britain's capacity to maintain her authority in the eastern Mediterranean. The causes were complex, but two stand out. The first was a positive decline in available resources. The second was the pace at which relations with the Arab world were changing. The first of these causes has been analyzed in other places and needs no repetition here. Its impact on the Mediterranean position of Great Britain can simply be noted as a fact. The second cause, however, is of Mediterranean origin and calls for fuller examination.

Great Britain had long accepted the need to revise her relations with the Arab world and to find a more realistic accommodation between her interests and the political aspirations of Arab nationalism.

Steps had been initiated to evolve a new status without destroying the achievements of the old and without interrupting the continuity of relations. In 1944 the British government had let it be known that it thought the time was ripe for the Arab states to concert common foreign policies and to adapt common measures for improving their economic and cultural relations. The first effort, made at the invitation of Egypt, had come to little; but the second, called at Cairo in February, 1945, pushed rapidly through to a covenant for an Arab League.

The meeting at Cairo was marked by the same traditional discords between Arab leaders that had prevented success at an earlier date; but this time the Conference worked to satisfy a pressure of expectancy that had been stimulated in Arab opinion. The League accordingly began its activities with a burden of unrealizable hopes, and most of its members were more concerned with the internal political liabilities thus acquired than with the real problems of the Middle East. The League became from the start a sounding board for agitating particular outstanding issues between Great Britain and its members, and did not develop procedures for peacefully adjusting the general relations between the Arab states and Great Britain. This had the effect of speeding up the pace at which change was being attempted and introduced uncertainty and intransigence into a situation that required time above all else for its handling.

Two issues, the revision of the Anglo-Egyptian Treaty of 1936 and of the Palestine Mandate, provided examples of the way in which the over-all British system of authority was being subjected to abnormally high pressures. The in-

decision and clamors with which both were handled measured the growing rabble-rousing techniques of the Arab
League and the growing sense of urgency on the British
side. In addition, through both issues, as well as through
general relations, ran the thread of a larger strategic problem.*

These strategic considerations, since they directly affected
the Anglo-American position, made evidence of weakness
on the part of Great Britain a matter of serious concern to
the United States. A structure of policy toward the Soviet
Union was being erected, and one of its supporting elements
was the combined position in the Mediterranean. Richard
Crossman, while ignoring many of the overtones of this relationship, catches its crude appearance. "The more threat-
ening the international situation, the greater the need for
this base [Palestine], and for relations of mutual confidence
between Britain and the countries in which these oil fields
lie. Equally, the greater the tension between America and

* The strategic interest of Great Britain in the Mediterranean consists
of specific points of control imbedded in a vast confusion of influence,
traditional values, heated debate, and ineradicable suspicion. The essential
present situation probably is that the specific points of control and the
operation of influence are not such reliable assets as they were twenty years
ago. They have not, however, become significant liabilities. Judgment is
accordingly suspended concerning them. Pending the stabilization of relations with the Soviet Union, some of their previous values have been
restored.

Mr. Bevin, speaking to the Commons, gave the present working estimate:
the only basis of association with Arab countries was that of friendship.
Mere force could not succeed; but friendship spread through the Moslem
world right down to India might succeed. The practical dangers had to be
weighed against the great hope of seeing the Middle East working as a
whole with the United Kingdom. However, Great Britain could be no
party to leaving a vacuum in the area. If she withdrew, it would be with
the knowledge that she was replaced by something. See Chronology of
International Events, II, x, May, 1946, p. 280.

The United States tacitly agreed to this estimate in 1946, and in 1947
was obliged openly to adopt it as its own understanding of the strategic
issues of the Mediterranean.

Russia, the greater the American interest in maintaining the British position in the Middle East which safeguards not only British but American oil." [1]

The fact was that the maintenance of the Anglo-American position, by becoming more and more essential to the support of American interests, raised large questions of policy. Either the established British system of authority and influence had to be underwritten or the United States had to face the necessity of developing an equivalent American system. The first choice was undesirable for many reasons. The second was impossible in view of the long-term planning and the backing from American opinion that it would require. The only workable compromise between the undesirable and the impossible was for the United States to relieve Great Britain in agreed sectors of their combined position. Early in 1947 a situation arose that required a decision either openly to accept the implications of this relationship or permanently to accept the consequences of its disruption. In February the British government privately informed the Department of State that its economic and financial condition was such that it could not allocate funds for the maintenance of stability in Greece after March 31. This announcement coincided with investigations then underway in Greece by an American Economic Mission and by a Commission of the United Nations. Early information from these investigations gave no grounds for hoping that Greece would stabilize itself. The alternatives were plainly presented: the United States accepted the responsibility of maintaining Greece as an element in the Anglo-American system of influence or it permitted Greece to become an element in a Soviet system of influence.

If the main line of American policy for the preceding eighteen months had been to resist the expansion of Soviet influence, to assert an American interest, and to prevent the disintegration of the European political system—and there is much to suggest that this was the basic course—then the position of Greece on one side or the other of the existing balance was a matter of importance. The argument stated that, if Greece fell into the hands of its Communist opposition, the political and military alignments of the whole region would fundamentally change. Turkey would become vulnerable. The Soviet Union would have access to the Mediterranean. British influence in the Middle East would receive an additional shock at a time when it was already weakening. The possible effect on the internal political balance of Italy could not be precisely calculated, but the worst was to be feared. A series of government meetings in Washington brought the rapid decision to accept a commitment to maintain the existing status of both Greece and Turkey as essential to American security and in the interest of European stability.*

The formal statement of the decision was made by President Truman on March 13, when he addressed Congress and recommended an appropriation of $400,000,000 for direct aid to Greece and Turkey. Behind the official generalizations lie the stages by which an American position, an American interest, had developed in the Mediterranean:

* This decision was interpreted, favorably and unfavorably, by the American press as a sign that the government was basing its policy on the facts of power relations. ". . . interest in Greece is not mere sentiment. Greece controls eastern Mediterranean strategy. Should Greece turn Communist, Turkey would be politically outflanked and could no longer resist a pressure that already is onerous. Without Turkey, Iran would go under. . . . Behind this pie-crust of three countries, linking Europe to Asia across the Hellespont, are fledgling Arab states without stability. The United States has a powerful concern . . . [where] there probably is more oil than in the United States' proved reserves."—C. L. Sulzberger, New York *Times*, March 5, 1947.

The foreign policy and the national security of this country are involved.

. . . a militant minority, exploiting human want and misery, was able to create political chaos.

Great Britain finds itself under the necessity of reducing or liquidating its commitments.

. . . assistance is imperative if Greece is to survive as a free nation.

The future of Turkey . . . is clearly no less important than the future of Greece.

That integrity is essential to the preservation of order in the Middle East.

Should we fail . . . the effects will be far reaching to the west as well as to the east.

This is no more than a frank recognition that totalitarian regimes imposed on free peoples, by direct or indirect aggressions, undermine the foundations of international peace and hence the security of the United States.[2]

One important aspect of the situation was not clearly stated. The inference was permitted that an unexpected crisis had been thrust upon the government. The facts, on the contrary, suggest that the United States had, by logically related steps, reached a point at which it had to choose between fairly clear alternatives. The decision it asked the American people to make was not whether they would accept new and unforeseen responsibilities, but whether they would confirm positions that had already been assumed and could not now be abandoned without leading to basic changes in the whole structure of the nation's international position. Only in this light does the proposal to maintain Greece and Turkey fall into proper perspective and escape the criticism of being a reckless improvisation.

XI. The Position

WHEN important centers of power disappear from a region where they have been influential, the relations of those powers that remain are subject to greater strain and become correspondingly less elastic. In the Mediterranean, where the early weakening of France was followed by the complete elimination of Italy, this characteristic of international relations was showing by the end of 1943. It conditioned the attitudes of Great Britain and the Soviet Union and, by an inevitable extension, those of the Soviet Union and the Anglo-American authority in the region.

The official American policy of trying to develop a system of international security that would work to modify this element in international relations did not provide an immediately available alternative. Though the objective was amply supported by public feeling and pressed with energy, events outran the slow processes by which the United Nations could be constructed. One of the most significant of these events was that Anglo-American authority in the Mediterranean developed the characteristics of a genuine center of power—a capacity to produce sensitive reactions in a neighboring center and a consciousness of pressures on itself.

This development is the essential starting point for an analysis of the present American interest in the Mediterranean. Though the interest of the United States in any region outside its continental limits is basically determined by factors that are external to the region itself, this feature of American policy is given extra emphasis, as far as the Mediterranean is concerned, by the fact that the United States had there become an active partner in the maintenance of a position of power. It was accordingly primarily concerned with using this position to support aims which lay beyond the boundaries of the region and with guarding against the actions of an external power that might threaten to undermine the position.

In what follows it will be necessary frequently to speak of the "use" that the United States will wish to make of its position in the Mediterranean region. The term will unfortunately suggest imperialism, exploitation, and a cold-blooded overriding of the interests of weak nations. Yet there is no good alternative way of indicating the fact that there are purposes which a nation tries to serve by the efforts and resources it expends beyond its own boundaries. The term "use" will be employed to express this fact. It would be a great mistake to assume that humanitarian objectives and a sincere regard for the liberties and national integrity of states so "used" are excluded. On the contrary, unless the methods of a police state or the techniques of terror are employed, effective "use" is now more likely to require a careful consideration of the interests and wishes of others than was the case when persuasion and co-operation were not so necessary to success.

As this concept of "use" is developed, a distinction must be made between those aims and purposes whose field of action lies outside the Mediterranean region but whose accomplishment depends in part on the maintenance of a position of power and influence within the Mediterranean and those aims and purposes that can be defined and pursued and achieved wholly within the region. The first group is illustrated by relations between the United States and the Soviet Union. The American position within the Mediterranean, as it is applied to these relations, is being applied to ends that fall outside the region. The second group is illustrated by relations between the United States and the Arab states. The development of these relations takes place primarily within the Mediterranean. Although the interdependence of these two groups of aims and purposes is obvious, American policy cannot be adequately examined unless it is possible to distinguish between them. The terms "external" and "internal" are used for this purpose. When American policy is primarily considering the Mediterranean, or any part of the region, as a means to an end that is not of direct concern to the region itself, "external" will be used. When American policy is considering the Mediterranean, or any part of the region, as an end in itself, "internal" will be used.

During the greater part of the war American interest was confined to maintaining a stable base for military operations against the Axis. In the closing stages of the war it was to provide leverage for maintaining the political and economic systems of adjacent areas. More recently, it has been to check the extension of a Communist-Russian influence. In each instance the Mediterranean was treated as a unit. The assumption that this could be done was validated by the completeness of Anglo-American control and by the success with which a minimum internal stability was preserved. At no time were the internal affairs of the Mediterranean region considered as important in themselves. They were important only as they might affect the use of the region as a unit. This habitual attitude was confirmed as the significance of the American position was more generally admitted. The use that could be made of the Mediterranean consistently took priority over the claims of such internal Mediterranean problems as forced themselves on official attention.

This one-sided approach, more to be noticed in American than in British thinking, could not be absolutely maintained. The relaxation of Anglo-American authority after the war permitted local claims to reassert themselves. In consequence, a policy of using the Mediterranean for external purposes became obviously dependent upon the existence of a policy which was concerned with the region's special needs and internal tensions. American policy was slow to grasp this relationship, although an understanding of its importance had long been second nature to Great Britain. British policy, while consistently emphasizing the external benefits of Great Britain's position in the Mediterranean, has always taken into account the necessity of keeping the region stable and usable.

In response to this need, an elaborate and organic system of authority, influence, and cultural and commercial ties grew up, co-ordinated with and yet separate from the policy by which Great Britain developed and supported her global interests. Internal and external considerations with respect to the Mediterranean region became so interlocked and so mutually dependent that their respective claims were adjusted and reconciled almost automatically.*

* The respective values of these claims were fundamentally debated only at moments of crisis. Italy forced such a moment in 1935-36 and a long argument followed between the Mediterranean and the Cape schools of strategy. The former, dismissing the concept of the Mediterranean as a life line, insisted that the real issue was the deterioration of Great Britain's global position that would follow if a vacuum were left in the Mediterranean by her withdrawal. Sir Samuel Hoare announced the government's decision: "We are quitting nothing. . . . For us the Mediterranean

The United States, starting in 1942, similarly emphasized the external values of a Mediterranean position, but it did not lay the foundations of a supplementary Mediterranean policy. This meant in effect that the region served American purposes chiefly because its internal stability was maintained by the British system of control. This was in accordance with the basic Anglo-American strategic agreement which specified the region as a political responsibility of Great Britain. This agreement tended to become unworkable in 1943, and mounting increments of material American support were thrown into the region. In the course of five years the original distinction was blurred in practice. When at the war's end it was officially reasserted, it was soon discovered that the separate maintenance of British and American interests was difficult. But experience of these difficulties did not lead to an anticipation of a possible need to develop an American policy and an American system of influence in the Mediterranean. The first real check came when the British announced that they must withdraw from Greece. The American reaction, in the form of the Truman Doctrine, produced a policy which contented itself with defining the external ends to be gained by maintaining Greek sovereignty. No mention was made of the fact that the more precise the commitment at any one point in the Mediterranean, the more essential it was to preserve the strategic unity and provide for the stability of the entire region.

To have recognized and acted on this necessity would have made the United States a direct participant in Medi-

is not a short-cut but a vital interest. . . ." The debate has been joined again in 1946-47. More complicated factors—limited resources, altered global interests, anti-imperial attitudes in the Labour Party—have entered into it. This time the United States is a deeply concerned follower of the argument.

terranean affairs and committed it to the same endless problem of adjusting external values and internal tensions that had long filled the files of the British Foreign Office. There was a despairing significance in Senator Hawkes' remark, made during the congressional debate on Greek aid: "I would have given England $400,000,000 and let her remain in there, because she knows, back through all history, the habits . . . and the intrigues of those people." A little acidly, *The Economist* pointed out that: "The Americans will find no responsibility in Greece. They must take what there is with them. They will find no policy in Greece save a mixture of sloth and violence. They must create the policy." [1]

Many difficulties, tangible as well as intangible, stood in the way of taking up such a burden. Opinion as well as tradition were against the principle of intervention that it implied. But, more practically, the American government was not organized for the rapid and continuous co-ordination that this type of self-perpetuating policy required. Relevant information and the freedom to make *ad hoc* decisions were so widely spread through the functional bureaus of the government that there was no inevitable point at which all Mediterranean problems would automatically meet for correlation and action.

Difficulties of this practical sort are not insurmountable, but they are usually surmounted only when the need is clearly seen and generally agreed upon. This was not at the time the case. Although the Mediterranean was employed as a unit by American policy, there was no sign that the region was consciously thought of as a single problem. Attention remained compartmentalized in terms of conventional political divisions (Spain, Italy, Greece, Palestine, or

Egypt), or in terms of functional bureaus (trade, finance, resources, strategy).

The inherent weakness of the situation has not yet been acutely felt. But as long as American security finds control of the Mediterranean region necessary, that condition cannot be steadily met unless there is a comprehensive policy for dealing with the Mediterranean itself. If the strategic values of the Mediterranean as they existed at the end of the war are exactly described, and if the American position there is set in an historical context, the importance of a concurrent policy will be more readily understood.

At the end of 1945 the Mediterranean was more under the control of a single agency than at any time since the division of the Roman Empire into its eastern and western parts. It was an Anglo-American domain. The greater part of its littoral was directly subject to Anglo-American control. Its hinterland, with the exception of the Balkans, was in uniform dependence upon the economic good will of these powers. The major approaches by way of the Straits of Gibraltar and the Red Sea were adequately held. The minor approach through the Dardanelles was still closed against egress from the Black Sea. The desert space between the Levantine coast and the borders of Afghanistan was effectively policed by air and road communications.

Other positive advantages existed. The region contained ample supplies of an essential raw material—oil. Climatically it offered optimum favorable conditions for air operations. It was well equipped with landing fields and ground facilities for air communications. Its harbors, while not ideally adequate, were developed to the point where they could support naval forces equal to any immediately foreseeable situation. There was no local industrial potential except in northern Italy and Spain, but the war had shown that this was not a disadvantage. Finally, the traditional British system of administration and authority, though weakening in many respects, was still in place and still operative. In no other region of comparable strategic significance did the United States possess so much at so little cost.

These advantages, however, were fully realizable only if the Mediterranean was treated as a unit and the interdependence of its parts recognized. Occasional inconsistency to the contrary, Anglo-American authority during the war assumed this interdependence and acted accordingly. But the unifying influence of this authority began to weaken after the war. Arab nationalism subjected its purely British element to increasing strain. French imperialism questioned its policy of seeking stability at the expense of French interests. Significant differences of judgment and action began to show between the United States and Great Britain. Finally an admitted weak spot in the structure began to develop into a sore spot. Yugoslavia, by rejecting its previous ties with Western Europe, permitted Russian influence to reach the shores of the Mediterranean. Thus, at a moment when internal stresses began to undermine the unity that Anglo-American authority had imposed, the need to use the region as a strategic unit continued to be as important as it had been during the war. For in the Balkans beyond the Greek frontier, Soviet methods hinted at the possibility that a union might be shaped that would represent the extension of the power centered in Moscow.

American policy, under these conditions, performed an act of faith in 1946 and 1947. A course of action was laid down as if this unity was an absolute fact. On this basis, immediate Soviet pressures and claims were resisted in Iran, in

Turkey, and in Greece. But there is ground for thinking that this firm line succeeded at the time rather because it was not seriously tested than because its foundations were solid.

The transfer of responsibility in Greece, Turkey, and Iran from Great Britain to the United States calls for a more comprehensive study of this question than it has yet been given. In each of these responsibilities lies the unstated implication of a possible resort to force. In this connection the internal coherence of the Mediterranean becomes of primary importance. American action in Greece presumes a minimum stability in Italy, and American action in Turkey and Iran presumes a minimum stability in the bordering Arab states. These stabilities are, in their turn, partially dependent on the course of events in France and Spain * and in more remote Arab-Moslem areas. The chain can be weakened by any number of factors at any number of places.

The American position in the Mediterranean is, in the last analysis, only as strong as the American policy for maintaining the internal stability of the Mediterranean is adequate. For the moment the gap between the two is not serious. A residue of Anglo-American control remains, and the forces of disunity are far from having developed their full impact. But as long as any gap exists, a course of action

* Policy with respect to Spain is a constant reminder that the position is sensitive. The United States since the war has consistently avoided supporting any action that might conceivably revive chaos in Spain, chaos being understood as a fluid situation that offered opportunities of exploitation to the Communist Party. This policy has never implied a positive support of General Franco. It is simply a recognition of the value of letting sleeping dogs lie. The drift toward the formation of a Western sphere in Europe, coupled with mounting commitments in the Mediterranean, now makes this policy seem necessary as well as desirable and encourages the search for ways of making it more palatable to public opinion.

which assumes the unity of the Mediterranean rests on an uncertainty and contains an irreducible element of bluff.

The success of the policy now being worked out in Western Europe depends in part on the maintenance of the present position in the Mediterranean. At some point in the development of this policy the pressure of Soviet power on the northern and eastern borders of the Mediterranean region will be more positively exerted. At such a time the American position there will be subjected to sharper testing than it has yet met with. This possibility becomes clearer if the situation is seen in its historical context.

Although the interplay of power interests in the Mediterranean has been extremely complex, only two elements have been persistently present during the past hundred and fifty years. These have been, first, the relation between the British position in the Mediterranean and the global position of the British Empire and Commonwealth, and, second, the existence of Great Britain and Russia as the two poles of power in the eastern Mediterranean. All other interests—French, Italian, Arab—were of a secondary order on any purely objective reckoning. The sole condition under which these two powers came together in a common cause was when it appeared possible that a third might establish itself in the region. Germany twice essayed this role in the twentieth century.

Between them Russia and Great Britain considered the Balkans and relevant sections of the Middle East as areas where the maximum security that either could hope to achieve was gained by preventing any stabilization that would favor the other's interests. In order not to be diverted from this major concern, Great Britain cultivated Italy and Spain as weak friendly nations and sought to identify the interests of herself and France in the western Mediterranean. The price of a French Empire in North Africa was paid in this connection.

The first World War seemed to have altered, in favor of Great Britain, this long-standing but precarious balance. With the Turkish Empire dismembered, and with Russia exhausted by revolution, the boundaries of British influence were pushed closer to the body of Russia than at any time since the Crimean War. The enforced quiescence of the Soviet Union prevented effective countermeasures. The same quiescence, however, permitted subordinate interests to develop.

Thus Turkey effected her reorganization as a local power, and Italy and France had time and space to maneuver. Simultaneously nationalism in the Arab world became a political force. Of all the secondary interests released, only those of Italy became a serious threat to Great Britain. Italian aspirations, by running counter to every interest that Britain defined as vital, provided one of the major false leads of the period between the wars. The defeat of Italy, though for a short moment it seemed to restore the British position as of 1919, in reality simply cleared the ground for the revival of the basic conflict between Russia and Great Britain. Signs of a vigorously renewed activity on the part of Soviet Russia soon followed.

The United States was awkwardly placed in relation to this conflict. It was on the one hand temperamentally and sincerely committed to tripartite agreement and to the development of an international system of security. It was, on the other, practically committed to a combined Anglo-American control of the Mediterranean. Finally, as it became clear that the foundations of international security depended on the rapid stabilization of Europe, preservation of the Anglo-American position in the Mediterranean took precedence. A great deal turned on the actual influence that the United States could bring to bear in Europe, and the readiest lever for this purpose was control of the Mediterranean.*

The unsuccessful attempt to use this position to check the expansion of Soviet power in the Balkans was balanced by its successful use to resist Soviet penetration into the Mediterranean. The fact, however, that the position was used at all had the effect of giving the Mediterranean the status of an important security interest in American eyes. Even a partial acceptance of this interest put the United States beside Great Britain in a precise strategic context.

The consequences of this alignment are not yet measurable because we are still in the very early stages of their development. But one or two general guesses can be ventured. The United States, for the immediate future, cannot avoid regarding the Mediterranean as a region of primary strategic importance. Although attention is momentarily fixed on the sector between Greece and Iran, the dependence of this sector on supporting positions to the west and south cannot be overlooked and the need to consider the stability of the entire region is instantly implied.

The obvious reaction to this implication is to use more fully and openly the existing British system of influence, supplementing it as required. This course, however, essentially leaves the problem of making internal adjustments in the Mediterranean in British hands and accepts the British

* Except in this region the distribution of actual American power in Europe after 1945 was neither strategically useful nor politically effective. And even in the Mediterranean its use in support of diplomatic action depended chiefly on the fact that it stood for a potential that could be rapidly made actual in the form of naval and air force.

estimate of the situation. In this lies its long-term weakness, for the extent to which Great Britain can make adjustments which will at the same time fit the realities of her global position and harmonize with the local Mediterranean interests of the United States is highly speculative.*

The only valid alternative to this in-between method of partially supporting and partially replacing the British system is for the United States to set up an equivalent American system and to develop a coherent and comprehensive approach to the Mediterranean as a whole. Theoretically there is something to be said in favor of this alternative as a long-term objective, but for the short run it is clearly impossible. It would require preparation over a long period of time (in the case of personnel alone, a generation of directed training would be needed), and it is plainly unrelated to any observable conviction in American public opinion. While there is always the hope that the problem of Mediterranean stability can be brought within the scope of the United Nations, this hope cannot be the sole basis for policy.

So American action in the Mediterranean is in part unilateral, in part an underwriting of the costs of maintaining a British system, in part a replacing of Great Britain in agreed sectors, and in part a co-ordination of parallel interests. The situation is absolutely clear at two points only. American power has deliberately interposed itself in Greece, in Turkey, and in Iran between the Soviet Union and British authority in

* In addition to economic difficulties, which have already made Great Britain less willing to carry this load for the United States, there is the possibility of a basic change in Britain's global strategy. Withdrawal from India has altered completely the strategic significance of the Suez Canal and opened the way for an examination of an alternative African position based on the Kenya-Nigeria-South Africa triangle. British policy might well accept a junior position in the Mediterranean in the interest of reconsolidating her position as a world power.

the Middle East. American influence, exercised directly in the form of loans and indirectly through plans to rehabilitate Western Europe, has become a key factor in the future development of Italy. In all other respects the situation is uncertain.

XII. The Interests of Others

SO much has been so loosely said of the Mediterranean interests of past and present powers that it is essential to clear this ground before coming to an estimate of American policy. Although any statement of the present interests of Great Britain, the Soviet Union, and the United States can be criticized from a hundred vantage points of special knowledge and preconceived opinion, the effort must be made. The relations of the external forces that play upon the Mediterranean are so unstable that all interested powers state their claims without limit and leave broad margins of ambiguity around their policies.

Since the historical interests of Great Britain have been so often reiterated, they constitute the starting place. These interests have consisted of gearing a Mediterranean position to a global position, of retaining the power to exert a direct influence in Europe from a position in the Mediterranean, and of exercising the maximum authority over the direction of political developments in the Mediterranean with the minimum commitment of actual power. In the course of time a highly diversified and widely spread commercial and financial interest was incorporated with these strategic and political interests.

All of these interests have been profoundly affected by the war, though the extent to which they have been modified or abandoned is a matter of argument and not of fact at the present moment. One thing, however, is certain: an imperial conception as voiced by Churchill is not the key to British thinking. His analysis of particular situations, and his reminders that geography, history, and human nature are not to be ignored, can be appreciated without necessarily assuming that his former policy decisions or his present policy judgments represent the line being followed. A revived imperialism is plainly not contemplated and is clearly not the temper of British opinion.*

What this means in terms of revisions of basic strategy is not clear to an outside observer, and perhaps not entirely certain to the British government. It suggests, however, that a fundamental reconsideration, based on more than doctrinal differences between the Labour and Conservative parties, may be under way. Financial difficulties may force the pace of change, but the grounds are more than economic.

The older strategy of the life line and the short cut, though in fact a dying concept for many years, can be dropped. The related strategy of influencing European affairs by the operations of sea power in the Mediterranean may also be of declining significance. One of the main channels by which that influence moved—the Balkans—is blocked. The other channel—Italy—though not blocked, is now more susceptible to American than to British guidance. In any case, this strategy of indirect influence stemmed from the position of Great Britain as a world power with European interests. There is now a good deal to be said for the view that sees Great Britain

* Mr. Bevin, speaking in the Commons on the Anglo-Egyptian negotiations of 1946, started from a different principle. "Relations with Egypt [have] rested on a very narrow basis; we have never gained the gratitude of the masses of the people. [We have] added great wealth to Egypt, but it [has] never flowed down to the *fellahin,* so [that] those with whom we dealt formed an extremely narrow circle."—*Chronology of International Events, loc. cit.*

basing her future on being a European power with world interests. If this change of front were ever decisively made and then deliberately implemented, British strategic interests in the Mediterranean would be altered beyond recognition.

But pending this or any other equally fundamental change, a current strategic interest remains. It has two aspects, a local and a general. Its local aspect is concerned with the defense of oil resources in Iran, Iraq, Trans-Jordan, and Saudi Arabia, and with the defense of refinery, pipe line, and port facilities in Syria and Palestine. Its general aspect is concerned with not permitting a vacuum to form in the Middle East as long as there is a possibility of that vacuum being filled by unfriendly power. The present assumption is that it would be filled either by the Soviet Union directly or by states subject to Soviet influence. The consequences of such a development are to be estimated not merely in terms of the British historical position in the Mediterranean, but on a world scale.

The question of Soviet Russia introduces the political interests of Great Britain. Formerly these were diversified and detailed, since on their proper handling depended the internal stability of the Mediterranean. The full range of influence, from intervention by force to discreet persuasion, was employed in forwarding these interests; and it was chiefly in this connection that the extensive British system of authority and administration was developed. These interests now seem to be reduced to two—a negative one of preventing a Communist-Russian influence from establishing itself, and a positive one of converting a system of semi-colonial control over the Arab states into a system of friendly co-operation with a regional group of sovereign Arab states. This shift is not only consonant with unavoidable trends, but prepares the way for safely changing basic strategic positions.* To carry out such a purpose with the minimum disturbance and with the maximum assurance that freely given co-operation would result is probably the major political interest that Great Britain now has in the Mediterranean.

The problem of moving safely through what may be a prolonged interim period is admittedly difficult. The course to be steered among the crosscurrents of nationalism, social maladjustment, economic necessities, and strategic considerations cannot be easily or surely charted. Its main bearing, however, is gradually becoming fixed. The distant objective is the establishment of a regime for the Middle East based on Arab nationalism and combining well-being and independence in its component parts with security and equal access to the whole for the major powers. But the distance between the present fact and this ultimate hope is enormous, and the road is sewn with booby traps. To hold on to older interests until newer ones have become clarified, to occupy positions while at the same time preparing to withdraw from them, is the most delicate of diplomatic operations.

The last general interest to be noted—the commercial and financial one—gives additional point to this problem. The greatest of these interests, and the one which comes closest to being vital, is the oil of the Middle East. Not only does it represent a large and profitable investment, but the British government, as a stockholder and as a guardian of strategic resources, is deeply committed to its defense. Other

* The idea of an Arab bloc is at least as old as Kitchener's proposals for the formation of a defensive chain of friendly Arab states. The conviction that British interests could be more profitably furthered by agreement and mutual consent than by coercion and control is at least as old as the lessons learned in the Syrian revolt of 1920. The steady growth of Arab nationalism has supported both.

commercial interests, though great, are essentially private, diversified, and firmly imbedded in the economic life of the Mediterranean. Their protection does not require a costly and extensive system of authority and administration. It does, however, require that the Mediterranean be a region of stable and co-operative governments.

But until there is some assurance that this condition will be met, Great Britain cannot lay down a course of action that includes the risk of being shut out of the eastern Mediterranean as both she and the United States have been shut out of southeastern Europe. Certainly a process of withdrawal that appears precipitous would increase this risk. Whatever may be the ultimate relationship contemplated by British policy, the interim objective of policy must be to slow down the pace at which change comes about. One of the methods of achieving this is to encourage the development of American interests and the growth of American power in the Mediterranean.

In comparison with the rich historical texture of British relations with the Mediterranean, those of the Soviet Union are simple and bleak. No economic interests can be noted, and no possibilities of fruitful economic exchange seem likely. Except for an immediate need resulting from the run-down condition of productive facilities in the Russian fields, the Soviet concern with the oil of the Middle East is a negative one, resting on the strategic value of denying it to other powers rather than on a vital need to acquire it.

Strategic interests are, however, precisely defined and vigorously pursued. Some of these interests have a long history: the control of the Straits, an expansionist drift toward India, and the establishment of a subordinate center of Slavic power in the Balkans. These were variously inter-

preted in the nineteenth century as defensive and expansionist. Imperial Russian diplomacy lent itself to either view.
The question is still undecided.

However, assuming for the moment that these historical
interests are being pursued for reasons of security, they have
been satisfied in southeastern Europe and they have been
frustrated in Turkey and Iran. On the other hand, taking
the Soviet interest in Tangier, Italy, and the Italian colonies
as expansionist, this effort to penetrate into the heart of the
Mediterranean was effectively resisted by the joint action of
the United States and Great Britain.

But in marked contrast to Soviet procedures in the Balkans
and on the borders of Turkey and Iran, these diplomatic
efforts to intervene in the distribution of power in the Mediterranean lacked the support of force and were not pressed.
They can be considered as having no more precise purpose
than to disturb British and American influence at any and all
points and to test the tolerance of Anglo-American policy.
Without attempting to decide whether or not such moves
indicate a dynamic and expansionist policy, it can be assumed
that the Soviet Union will continue to make them. The more
exactly an American interest is defined, and the more that
interest seems to be identical with, or to give support to,
British interests, the more positive are Soviet pressures likely
to become and the more tenaciously will they be maintained.
Short of being included in a clear settlement of all the
difficulties now outstanding between the United States and
the Soviet Union, there is no reason to expect a reduction of
these pressures. Their continuation is obviously more costly
to the United States and Great Britain in terms of energy,
attention, and resources than it is to Russia.

On the political side, Soviet purposes are difficult to

specify. The desirability of controlling the course of political developments in Italy, Greece, Turkey, and Iran is obvious, for in these areas strategic aims and political control are interlocked. But beyond these limits the situation is confused, and it is to the benefit of the Soviet Union that it should remain so. A purely Russian interest, in the sense of an adaptation of an older imperial Russian aim, slides through fine intermediate stages into a Communist interest, and the Soviet Union becomes involved in supporting the forces of social and political disintegration on principle and not necessarily for definable national ends.*

The interests of certain subordinate powers can now be added. The common feature of these secondary interests is that their pursuit directly affects the internal stability of the Mediterranean. They are, in order of their present importance, the interests of France, of the Arab League, of Italy, and of the Balkan states. All of these interests have been overstated in the past, and at least the French and Arab ones are overstated in the present.

Except for Greece, the Balkan states are not inevitably Mediterranean powers. They make up an area which can be either a Mediterranean hinterland or an outpost of central Europe and Russia. It can and has acted both roles at the same time. French and Italian policy between the wars followed lines which, if successful, would have drawn these states into the Mediterranean picture. This development was

---

* As a result of the uncertain boundary between doctrine and national interest, embarrassing choices are often forced on Soviet policy. Such cases have arisen in connection with the Marshall Plan and with the United Nations proposal to partition Palestine. In the former, communism in Italy and France is supported at the expense of relations with the two nations. In the latter, it must be presumed that the chance to participate directly in a Middle Eastern situation is considered more valuable than the cultivation of the Arab League.

effectively blocked by Germany in the preparatory stages of the war, and is equally blocked by the Soviet Union at the present moment. Yugoslavia and Bulgaria, in spite of their nationalistic insistence on interests in the Adriatic and the Aegean seas, are actually the fringes of Soviet influence. Their interests in the Mediterranean have force only as they are spearheads for the interests of the Soviet Union.

Italy, whose previous claims were inflated far beyond her power to support them, now offers a problem rather than a set of interests. At the core of fascist exaggeration was a vital national concern. It was defined by Grandi in 1932, and his statement is still valid: "Italy must also place a problem before the world . . . a problem which is directly connected with our future, a problem of undisturbed peace and of the work of a nation of forty-two millions. . . . How could these millions live . . . compressed into a territory half the size of France, Spain, or Germany, with no supplies of raw materials and no possibility of renewing their stocks . . . ? This problem . . . arises of itself and must form part of the great problem of international reconstruction. . . ." [1] This problem, intact and unsolved, has now passed to the United States and Great Britain. To attempt to solve it must continue to be a major aim of any Italian government, but it is a problem that can only be dealt with by Anglo-American means. For this reason it must be put down as an Anglo-American concern, under the general heading of factors affecting the internal stability of the Mediterranean.

French interests in the Mediterranean, in spite of a tradition of spacious definition, have in fact been concentrated on using the region to counterbalance France's weakening position as a continental power. From this was derived a formula which saw the empire in Africa as a reservoir of manpower and a means of defense in depth. On this formulation French policy staked everything, concentrating on the strategic domination of the line of communication with North Africa and on the absolute economic control of Tunisia and Algeria. The position and claims of France in the Levant were never specified as vital.

From the French point of view her interests in the Mediterranean have not changed. They have, however, become more difficult to support. French prestige in the Arab world is dangerously low and her control of the indigenous Arab population in North Africa and Morocco has been adversely affected. Yet France is more convinced than ever of the absolute need to hold what is hers in these areas, and her reaction to immediate difficulties is a policy of almost unrepentant imperialism. The application of such a policy in North Africa and Morocco is of more importance now than would previously have been the case, for it irritates Arab opinion generally and interferes with the development of favorable attitudes toward the West. It is thus a source of political instability along the entire southern coast of the Mediterranean.

The Arab interest must be thought of not in terms of the local concerns of the various Arab states, but as it is stated in the objectives of the Arab League. In spite of the fact that the aims of the League are a composite of aspirations, memories, dreams, broad political goals, and precise political targets, they are held together by a hard center of purpose. This purpose is to consolidate, on racial, religious, and nationalistic grounds, a self-contained and self-supporting Arab-Moslem community from Morocco to Iran. In pursuing this end the League is uninhibited by apprehensions of practical difficulty and steadily seeks to maneuver its Western European overlords into the retreats that will bring the ideal perceptibly nearer.

In actual fact, the League does not possess the means to carry out such a policy. It possesses merely a nuisance value in relation to the total situation in the Mediterranean. Its power resources are inadequate to forcing any of the issues involved, and its internal coherence has not yet been seriously tested by resistance to its claims. In the immediate future this interest cannot be developed against the opposition of Great Britain and the United States except by sacrificing the co-operation which the Arab League needs if it is to acquire any of the genuine attributes of power. The Arab world, however, stirred by nationalism, urged by religious faith, and driven by xenophobic impulses, is capable of choosing even a destructive course and believing the world well lost. For this reason it is necessary to take into account a movement which can call such compelling forces into action.

XIII. The American Interest

THE interests of the United States in the Mediterranean are difficult to pin down. The excitements of war and the uncertainties of the future have led to a good deal of hasty assertion; if a list of interests were compiled on the basis of recent public statements it would be extensive. But when these claims are examined they can be considerably reduced without seeming to affect national security.

The bedrock of American relations with the Mediterranean region is cultural and commercial. American religious and educational establishments have a long history in the Levant and have put the United States in good standing with the Arab world. They now represent much more than the humanitarian impulses that founded them. They are a valuable asset and their protection and encouragement by proper means is a national interest.

Commercial contacts developed fitfully over a century and then expanded rapidly between 1930 and 1940. During the war American equipment and resources played a large part in improving the productive capacity of the Mediterranean region. The demand for American goods was so great that private hopes of a permanent new market were raised. Even before the war was over, the American government was being pressed to protect so valuable an asset.*

---

* A characteristic example can be found in the report of Senators Tunnel and Burton, made after a journey to the Mediterranean in 1943. They called for "a clear statement of American rights and interests in the

In 1943 these vague commercial anticipations were lifted to a higher level. American oil companies, which had been slowly working their way into the fields of the Middle East over a long period, came to satisfactory working agreements with established British companies and looked forward to a vast expansion in the near future. A much more precise and important interest was immediately definable. Furthermore, though essentially a commercial interest, it tended to become identified with strategic considerations.

For years American companies had tried to persuade the American government to come into their activities in order to counterbalance the participation of the British government in British companies. The Department of State had consistently avoided official involvement. But in 1943 the U.S. Joint Chiefs of Staff and other government bureaus became alarmed at the drain on domestic petroleum reserves. A broad general study was made and it was concluded that the economic as well as the strategic security of the United States required that this drain be checked. An expansion of production in the Middle East was strongly recommended. The emotionalism that always accompanies the discussion of petroleum resources hurried some departments of the government on to the point where they sketched a policy that included buying out privately held concessions in the Middle East.

The Department of State did not concur in this proposal. It argued that such a step "might incline the American government to shape its decisions on Middle Eastern affairs on wrong grounds." The supporters of the proposal replied

Mediterranean," adding that "the United States may be in serious danger of being entirely eliminated from world trade in that area."—*Congressional Record*, February 15, 1945, Vol. 91, No. 29, pp. 1160, 1219-28.

that, in the interests of American trade, the government must exert itself to compete with Great Britain and to counter-balance Russian influence: from a security point of view, "the United States had so vital an interest in the future of the region that it would find itself compelled to enter the struggle for influence; . . . it should, therefore, put itself in a position to make its views effective. . . ." [1] President Roosevelt finally approved the proposal and negotiations were opened.

At this point the companies which wanted government protection, not government ownership, withdrew. The opinion of the Department of State prevailed not on its merits, but because negotiations broke down. But as a result of the general discussion, the terms "vital interest," "dangerous depletion of an essential resource," and "national security" were vigorously publicized. The oil of the Middle East appeared as more than a commercial interest; it became a factor in the security of the United States. In this form it joined up with the general strategic interests which the United States developed in the Mediterranean.*

Aside from the particular pressure exerted by the wish to control or safeguard so valuable a resource as petroleum, it is clear that the interests of the United States in the Medi-

---

* In many respects the subject has reduced itself to ordinary economic dimensions since 1943-44, and the question of its being a vital interest has been examined with more detachment than was then possible. The present expert judgment appears to be that, though it is highly desirable for the United States to develop a policy of conserving domestic resources by every means at its disposal, particularly by expanding production in the Middle East, it does not follow that the Middle East reserves are a vital interest in the sense that military resources must be specifically earmarked for their defense under all conditions.

See Feis, *op. cit.*, p. 184 *ff.*, and Bernard Brodie, *Foreign Oil and American Security*, Yale Institute of International Studies, 1947, Memorandum No. 23.

terranean region differ fundamentally from those that have
been sketched for both Great Britain and the Soviet Union.
The essential point of difference is that the United States has
never been and is not now a Mediterranean power. The
United States has no direct interests within the Mediterranean region comparable to those Great Britain would wish
to defend or to those the Soviet Union might hope to develop.
The United States at the present moment is vitally concerned
only with the external purposes that can be served by maintaining a position of power and influence within the region,
and with the benefits that can be gained by keeping the Soviet
Union and Soviet influence out of the region. Any additional
claim that is staked out in the Mediterranean must be carefully examined to make sure that it is truly national and
must prove its validity by showing that it will support the
interests noted above.

Naturally these external objectives imply judgments and
decisions about the internal affairs of the Mediterranean, and
their realization depends in part on understanding and attempting to lessen the tensions that shape the course of these
affairs. But the United States has no specific internal interest
of a compelling kind. The actual course that America takes
in the Mediterranean should depend upon the judgment it
makes of the region's usefulness in other respects. On the
basis of the use that the United States has already made of
its position in the Mediterranean, the points of reference for
such a judgment are: first, what degree of influence will it
permit America to exert in support of its aims in continental
Europe; and second, what is its relation to the global position
of the United States? But at best such judgments are bound
to vary with changing circumstances and to give rise to

sharply divergent opinions. Mediterranean policy is accordingly hard to define.

Yet the feeling is strong that a very significant interest does exist, at least in the Middle East. This feeling is understandable since in this sector contacts with the Soviet Union are immediate, strategic issues are acute, and an economic interest has been vigorously established. American opinion, even though it could not clearly say how its conviction was to be converted into action, would be inclined to accept Speiser's statement that "No major power today can afford to dispense with an active interest. . . . The United States cannot surrender by default her right to determine whether it shall be peace or war [in the Middle East] any more than can Russia or Britain." [2] In spite of this general feeling no American policy for the Mediterranean has yet been formulated. Attention remains primarily focused on the external ends that can be served from a position on the Mediterranean.

In a general way the position of the United States in the Mediterranean in 1947 is reminiscent of that of Great Britain in the late eighteenth century. The essential reason for being there is that it gives a foothold for achieving desired ends elsewhere. As in the earlier case of Great Britain, the value of the foothold depends on the proper and favorable disposition of local relations and involves a limited concern with their general character. But this is a secondary even if necessary consideration. Only so much attention is spared for the subordinate problems of the Mediterranean as events demand.

The ends which the United States pursues by way of the Mediterranean are a blend of political and strategic considerations. As a result of the indefinable relationship between international communism and Russian nationalism, these ends can be expanded to a world scale or contracted to a European scale. The unique geographical position of the Mediterranean brings it into account on both scales. It is rarely clear by which of these scales American opinion is judging, but at the moment the scale is apparently European.

American policy with respect to Europe appears to be two-pronged. On the one hand it seeks to re-establish Western Europe as a self-supporting center of power. On the other hand, since Soviet Russia and international communism are believed to oppose this purpose, it seeks to check any and all activities that might prevent its realization. The ultimate end sought by this policy is not of concern here, though it can be assumed that it does not look to a single end, but merely to the opening up of multiple possibilities. The policy may lead to a more effective basis for an international security organization. It may equally lead to a world in which the United States and the Soviet Union are the only focuses of power. Or it may lead to a more stable type of balance in the world by encouraging the re-creation of strong and independent "in-between" powers.

In the preliminary and during the early stages of implementing a European Recovery Program the Mediterranean plays a definite part. Two obvious links exist between the American position there and American policy for Europe. These links are Italy in the west and Greece and Turkey in the east. Italy falls both inside and outside the Mediterranean. It is, on the one hand, a part of the Western Europe that is to be recovered and, as such, it will be subject to influences and controls from the north. But it is at the same time an integral part of the strategic unity of the Mediterranean and cannot be taken out of this context. It is peculiarly subject to Communist pressure both internally from its own Communist party and externally by way of Yugoslavia. In the American view it is essential that both types of pressure should be resisted and an intention to aid in such resistance has been stated.* Assistance to enable the Italian government to stand up against internal pressure would probably resemble that already given to France for the same purpose—encouragement and subsidy of the existing political authority; but assistance in resisting external pressure must envisage an ultimate willingness to use force. Thus Italy becomes a point of strategic tension from which the United States cannot easily withdraw its attention.

Greece and Turkey come entirely within the Mediterranean, but because they form an area in which Soviet power directly presses on the American position, they have been given a high priority of attention. Their significance is strategic, and their value in this respect is frankly acknowledged. In fact their continued independence has been explicitly defined as a vital American interest. At the time this definition was made it was accompanied by the hope that the mere act of definition might serve to shake the Soviet hold in southeastern Europe.

This hope has not been realized. On the contrary, the Soviet position has been more firmly consolidated. The frontier from Greece, through Turkey, and into Iran is less fluid now, less open to favorable stabilization in the American interest, than it was when the Truman Doctrine was an-

* Consider President Truman's statement of December 13, 1947, on the occasion of the withdrawal of American troops from Italy: "If . . . it becomes apparent that the freedom and independence of Italy . . . are being threatened directly or indirectly, the United States . . . will be obliged to consider what measures would be appropriate. . . ."—New York Times, December 14, 1947.

nounced. Primary consideration is consequently given to the use that can be made of the Mediterranean to restrain Russia within her boundaries in the Middle East and to check the expansion of Soviet influence into the Mediterranean generally. This external end can be sought simultaneously with such internal objectives as economic reconstruction or such general purposes as the hope of starting a "chain reaction" against totalitarian influences; but, regardless of how it is pursued, the external objective takes precedence over all other considerations.

The immediate consequence of failure in the external objective would be to endanger the Anglo-Amercian control of the oil resources of the Middle East. The remote consequences would be a profound modification of the existing strategic balance between Great Britain, the Soviet Union, and the United States. On the other hand, unless it can be incorporated into other and more general objectives, success in restraining and checking the Soviet Union achieves little beyond keeping the situation as it now is. It will not begin to solve the internal problems of the Mediterranean region. It will merely provide a favorable atmosphere for their solution.

This analysis of the main characteristics of the American interest in the Mediterranean leads to one question. If there are purposes for which the United States intends to make use of its position there, what is required to make that position solid, sure, and reliable? All that has been said up to this point prepares the ground for this question. All that follows is an attempt to answer it fully.

The factors that enter into the answer have already been suggested. The first is the necessity of treating the entire region as a unit. The second is the necessity of relying to a considerable extent on an existing British system of authority in the region. The third is the probable need to develop a comprehensive policy for maintaining the region's internal stability.

XIV. Internal Tensions

TO use the Mediterranean as a unit is a separate thing from trying to maintain its internal stability. The concept of the unit is primarily strategic and stands for the point of view of an outside power. In this view, internal stability is important only as it affects the serviceability of the region. Historically, the degree of stability required was achieved in the Mediterranean by a variety of methods: direct force, policing, political manipulation, permitting the growth of subordinate powers with complementary interests, developing economic, political, and cultural links, and finally persuasion and co-operation.

In general, as the texture of relations became richer, the direct application of force declined and the use of persuasion increased. The list of workable methods is smaller now than in the past. Force is more likely to defeat its ends than to gain them. New loyalties—nationalism and racism—have reduced the easy possibilities of political manipulation. The more usual contemporary technique is the development of mutual interests, supported by persuasion rather than threats. Thus the methods of preserving stability have grown in complexity.

The concept of the strategic unit is not wholly artificial. There is a basic uniformity imposed by geography and climate on the Mediterranean, and there are trends which work throughout the region to create similar problems of social and political adjustment. The Mediterranean is a geographical entity in which factors producing diversity and factors asserting uniformity are in perpetual concealed conflict. The centrifugal force of different patterns of culture and history and the centripetal pull of climate and economy are equally noticeable.

The particular equilibrium reached during the past century, though made familiar by experience and habit, is neither inevitable nor final. Other equilibriums were reached in the past, and it must be said of these older ones that they were more a consequence of the basic characteristics of the region than is the present one. The present one is a product of relations between external powers.

Some of the most significant uniformities in the Mediterranean derive from natural forces working on human material. Between the northern limit of the olive and the southern limit of the date palm, strikingly similar uses of the soil have developed and a surprisingly uniform agricultural economy has resulted. Landholding, land use, and the relation of peasant masses to the land—no matter how differently expressed in Spanish, Italian, Balkan, or Arab law and custom—is based either on a pattern of feudally worked large estates or on the gardening of small plots. Scattered centers of rationalized agriculture in the tobacco areas of Greece, the fruit areas of Palestine, the cotton areas of Egypt and the Sudan, and the olive and wine areas of Tunisia and Algeria have scarcely disturbed ancient practices. Other uniformities result from evenly distributed disadvantages of inadequate water, limited and undiversified raw materials, and populations pressing with unrelieved heaviness on the usable land. These similarities are at least as characteristic of the Mediterranean as are its more often remarked cultural and political dissimilarities.

Even cultural and political diversification has not always been as pronounced as it now is. From the seventh to the eighteenth centuries the Mediterranean was generally understood to be not a region of political fragments, but a broad frontier zone between the Christian world of Europe and the Moslem world of the Levant and Africa. It was equally understood that the region as a whole oscillated slowly between periods of being "closed" and periods of being "open" as it was or was not an available route of world trade. A notable period of "openness" came with the rise of the Italian city-states between 1100 and 1450. As *entrepôts* between the East and the West they developed commercial intercourse along and across a clearly recognized frontier.

The establishment of Turkish power at Constantinople in 1452 closed the trade routes again and re-emphasized the frontier character of the Mediterranean. Pressure to reopen the region did not develop, for alternative ocean routes were found for world trade. Except for the expansion of the Turkish Empire into the Balkans, the Mediterranean remained a "closed" region until French and British sea power in the eighteenth century discovered new uses to which it could be put.*

It is essential to realize that many of the present features which the Mediterranean shows were in great part imposed upon it from without. External forces broke the old frontier and peopled the region with impotent sovereignties, but it cannot be assumed that they have fundamentally changed

* To complete this picture reference should be made to the view of the Mediterranean built up by Italian policy during the fascist regime. In this view, which evoked the Mediterranean of the Roman Empire, the region was neither a trade route nor a frontier, but a unit controlled by a single power centered within it. As such it was a core from which power thrust out in all directions.

the bedrock of uniformity. Nor can it be taken for granted
that a frontier zone may not be again set up. The simultane-
ous development of a Communist-Soviet system in Western
Europe and of an integrated system of Arab states in the
Middle East and North Africa would set the stage for
redrawing a line of demarcation.

These hidden sources of unity suggest that the equilibrium
of the Mediterranean depends upon more than a control of
the region's diverse internal conflicts. It is a reminder that
these conflicts occur in a context that is not entirely con-
trollable by external powers. Still, it is the diverse internal
conflicts that occupy the foreground of attention and make
up the daily problem of British and American relations with
the Mediterranean.

The present internal tensions of the region show themselves in a variety of forms and on different scales of importance. Some are internal to individual states, some appear
as conflicts of interest between states and groups of states.
Others are more comprehensive ideological differences which
operate, in various guises, over large sectors of the Mediterranean. And finally there are some which result from the
general operation of long-term demographic and economic
trends. The success of any policy designed to stabilize the
Mediterranean depends upon finding the common factors in
the region's conflicts regardless of the forms in which they
show themselves. The form of such a policy must plainly be
regional.

It must shape itself in terms of essential trends and common problems and must handle a multiplicity of local issues
as variations on a few basic themes. To take an instance, the
pressure of population on the agricultural resources of Sicily
and of Egypt leads to social instability at these two points.

In the case of Sicily, the pressure is turned into a struggle against local landowners and is expressed in communist terminology, or alternatively becomes part of a separatist movement against the central authority of Rome. In the case of Egypt, it tends to get converted into a mass xenophobia which then becomes a factor in Egyptian political life and passes from there into the activities of the Arab League. In so far as these instabilities are a matter of concern to an external power, the question arises of whether they can be more effectively handled as separate and unrelated manifestations in local politics or as derivatives of a single demographic trend. The former method spells involvement in the indistinguishable rights and wrongs of irrelevant local controversies. The latter method appears better suited to the requirements of an external power interested in reaching a general solution with the minimum means.

The record of American experience in Greece gives confirmation. Even after all that can be said about the distorting effect of civil war has been accepted, the fact still remains that the essential sources of instability in Greece were not uncovered in the analysis of the situation that was made for the purpose of allotting funds. The problem was approached as if it were an isolated and local difficulty when in fact it was part of a regional problem locally complicated by civil war and outside pressures. In consequence, the American administrators of the policy of assistance were without broad points of reference and were compelled to use those that seemed locally significant.*

The value of carefully examining these alternative methods

* The best short survey of the situation for those who do not wish to piece together its elements from official reports and from the New York Times is "Knife Edge in Greece," in The Economist, July 5, 1947.

is emphasized if a rapid survey is made of the present sources
of instability in the Mediterranean. To begin at the level of
individual states, each is in a condition of social and political
tension whose roots lie deeper than the dislocations caused by
the war. Although the actual form varies from repressive
control in Spain and French North Africa, through political
competition between groups of the Right and the Left in
Italy and Greece, to unfocused revolutionary pressures in
Egypt, all conform roughly to the same pattern. In each state
there are growing maladjustments between the interests,
claims, and powers of landowners and increasing peasant
populations. In each state there is a declining rate of agricultural production in relation to the number of persons
dependent upon the land for their livelihood. In each state
a retarded industrialization makes it impossible to absorb
excess manpower into other productive work. In each state,
with the exception of Italy before the war, the application of
foreign capital to these problems was undirected and served
to freeze maladjustments rather than to cure them.[1]

The Arab states of the Middle East present a special
variation of this type of tension. To the general pattern is
added a particular conflict between the nomadic herdsman
and the settled cultivator. The interests of these two groups
are historically incompatible, and the equivalent of a double
political structure within the same state is needed to reconcile
their interests.* Italy and Spain also show special variations

* King Ibn Saud's projects in Saudi Arabia—if Antonius is correct in
his estimate of them—aim at resolving this tension by a progressive settlement of his nomadic subjects on the land. "An area of land adjoining . . .
water was assigned in freehold to a tribal group, [and was] to be their
fixed and permanent home. . . . They were to be provided with housing,
implements and guidance in the arts of systematic cultivation and cattle-
breeding; . . . each of these new colonies was . . . more or less self-

in consequence of the existence of highly industrialized areas whose activities are not geared to the national economy but rather to that of Western Europe. The irreconcilability of the interests of these small areas with the predominantly agricultural economy of the rest of the nation has contributed to separatist movements. In Spain the section around Barcelona has been a driving force in Catalonian separatism. In Italy the agricultural economy of Sicily and the South draws away from the administrative indifference of a government that is conventionally assumed to be acting in the industrial interest.

While it is true that the tensions here mentioned are invariably met with in their local forms, the interest of an external power cannot be adequately guarded if they are treated solely as local issues. They must at least be examined in relation to their general causes if a policy of intervention and manipulation is to be avoided.

The local approach is equally inadequate in the face of broad ideological sources of conflict. Two such operate in large areas of the Mediterranean without regard to local boundaries. In the Middle East and Africa a persistent tension exists between the Moslem concept of human relations and social organization and the concepts that are conventionally identified as "Western materialism." This tension is fully blended with a related conflict between Arab national-

contained in its local administration and economy."—G. Antonius, *The Arab Awakening*, Lippincott, 1939, p. 348.

On the other hand, a more detached authority points out that each Arab state in the Middle East pursues its own unco-ordinated policy in this respect and thus undermines isolated efforts to deal with the problem. The nomads merely move from areas where they are being improved to areas where they can more freely follow their traditional tastes. *See* H. A. R. Gibb, "The Future for Arab Unity," *The Near East*, Harvard University Press, 1947, p. 90.

ism and what is conventionally called "Western imperialism." In the Balkans and along the northern shore of the region an equally persistent tension has developed between two antagonistic social concepts—democracy and communism. It must not be forgotten, however, that these terms conceal more than they disclose of the historical, economic, and political forces that enter into their opposition in the Mediterranean.*

Frequent mention is made of the possibility of these two ideological movements—communism and Arab nationalism— joining forces in order to reach a common goal: the destruction of the existing *status quo* in the Mediterranean. There is some evidence of Soviet attempts to this end in the Middle East. Observers of these efforts, however, are inclined to report them as if they were accomplished fact. Momentary tactical co-operation is certainly possible between Arab nationalism seeking to escape from the authority of the West and Russian communism seeking to weaken the strategic position of Great Britain and the United States, but there is no natural compatibility between Moslem and Communist goals. No political party in the Arab world, except a small Communist group, proposes more than a temporary combination; to go further would merely exchange one alien authority for another. Actual Communist groups in Arab politics have a nuisance value but lack the strength and the

* In Italy and Spain, for example, the tension is both heightened and confused by including a special conflict between a doctrinaire anticlericalism and the social authority of the Catholic Church. In the Balkans it is heightened and confused by racial and cultural antagonisms and by remnants of tribal loyalties. It was frequently pointed out to the author in private conversations in both Greece and Bulgaria that the Bulgars would always join forces with the Russians even though they were Communists, while the Greeks had no profound objection to communism except that so many Communists were Slavs.

revolutionary *élan* of a genuine fifth column. If communism effectively penetrates the Middle East it will be on the heels of a Soviet expansion by force of arms. All other signs of its presence are significant only in the context of an Arab-Moslem struggle against "Western imperialism."

A more accurate estimate of the situation sees these two forces working, for the most part, separately: the one concentrated in the Middle East but reaching out along the African littoral, the other most strongly fixed in the Balkans but reaching out exploiting fingers to the Middle East and Africa.

It would be a serious mistake for an external power with Mediterranean interests to attempt to meet these intangible forces in their purely local manifestations. It is an accurate measure of their total strength and importance that is essential. Estimates based on local experiences invariably exaggerate the force of the movements in question and lead to disproportionate reactions.

The next group of conflicts belongs to a different category. It consists of the more conventional antagonisms that are peculiar to the Mediterranean. Most of them have historical foundations and, in the past, took on significance as they were caught up in the competing interests of external powers. Some have become inactive with the exclusion of subordinate powers from the region. Thus the eastern Mediterranean is no longer an area of Franco-Italian competition. But most of these conflicts still operate: most notably, long-standing controversies between the Balkan states; less well-known, dynastic competition in the Arab states.

The first set of controversies consists of irritating issues between Greece and Bulgaria in Thrace, between Greece and its Balkan neighbors in Macedonia, and between Yugoslavia and Italy in the Adriatic Sea. Competing claims to ports, strategic boundaries, and minorities have long passed the point at which they can be settled by negotiation. Nor can a settlement be imposed by agreement among external powers because the local points of contention have themselves become elements in the strategic thinking of the external powers. Their restatement in terms of Anglo-American-Soviet relations has, more than any other consideration, kept the Greek frontier and the area around Trieste lively issues. In these cases a regional policy for the Mediterranean would be obliged deliberately to take account of local factors. Tension is concentrated at points where long-range consequences are also involved, and to maintain immediate stability without prejudicing future hopes depends in considerable part on a shrewd appreciation of the local situation and its historical content.

The second set of conflicts, those that exist within the Arab world, does not directly affect the relations of the United States and Great Britain with the Soviet Union. Their significance lies in the fact that they determine the character and strength of the Arab League. The front which the League presents in international affairs is only as solid as the compromise of purely Arab interests on which it rests. But by way of the Arab League, the Arab states which individually play only a small role in the world become important. As a potentially coherent force their joint response to either Russian or Anglo-American influence becomes full of meaning. If the league of Arab states should equally resist both influences and establish itself as a separate center of power, this would also be an international development of great interest. Such a development would not necessarily be against the American and British interest, though it would not be as satisfactory as an Arab world closely linked in self-interest to the Western powers. As long as this group of states is not subject to Russian direction the major need of the moment is taken care of.

But the Arab states are not yet the Arab League in the sense that they constitute a coherent center of power. In the most favorable view they are in the preliminary stages of aspiration. At first sight, therefore, it would seem that relations with the Arab world could be best conducted in the form of diversified contacts with separate units. Certainly no one but an expert in Arab affairs can hope to estimate the exact relations between King Ibn Saud and the Hashimite rulers of Iraq and Trans-Jordan, whose dynastic forbear, Husein, was ousted from the Kingdom of Hejaz in 1924 by Ibn Saud himself. Equally difficult to assess are competing claims to the spiritual leadership of the Moslem world. And no one, not even an expert, can reliably guess at the shifting balance within the Arab world in consequence of the growing strength of those rulers who have oil royalties at their disposal.

Closer examination, however, shows that the diversified local approach is full of pitfalls. Too exclusive a reliance on local contacts makes policy a participant in an intense conflict of tribal feuds and dynastic discords. The greatest skill in dancing on eggs does not automatically produce a good omelet nor does the finest skill in conducting relations with separate Arab states automatically serve essential national interests. If the national interests of the United States are not confused with particular interests in the oil of the Middle East, it will be seen that they rest upon relations with the Arab world, not upon the sum of relations with a multiplicity of Arab states. The present situation of Great Britain, whose relations with individual Arab states are based upon a remarkable foundation of specialist knowledge, provides a clear illustration of how inapplicable this knowledge is to the general problem of relations with the Arab world.*

A reasonably firm conclusion can be drawn at this stage in the analysis. The genuine national interest which the United States has in maintaining its present position of power in the Mediterranean is in considerable part dependent on the internal stability of the region. A supplementary policy, concerned chiefly with the sources of instability within the Mediterranean, is consequently called for. Such a supplementary policy should be developed on a broad regional basis and should be designed to build up a set of relations whose cumulative impact on the complex structure of Mediterranean life will set the whole system moving in a direction compatible with American aims.

A minimum stability can probably be achieved by other means. It can be imposed, as it was during the war, by the unstinted application of resources in the form of subsidies and of pressures in the form of military power. But essentially these are devices for the short term only. Their excessive costs are usually supportable only in an atmosphere of crisis. A long-term policy would wish to reduce and spread the burden as much as possible. If this is translated into a course of action it means that the internal stability of the

* ". . . the far-reaching interdependence of the local states and territories imposes . . . [an] obligation to approach the entire region as a unit. To deal with one local state is to invite the intimate participation of the rest. And to pursue an economic objective in one part of the region is to be involved in the political life of the whole . . . policy . . . which is not a comprehensive regional policy is an invitation to bankruptcy." Speiser, *op. cit.*, p. 226.

This conclusion, though reached for the Middle East, is equally valid for the Mediterranean as a whole.

Mediterranean can be most surely and cheaply maintained if the region can be put in the path of developing its own resources to this end. Effective influence in this direction is not the product of a sum of local contacts; it is the consequence of a consistently operating regional policy.

XV. Demography and Economics

TWO important and widespread sources of instability remain to be described: a marked trend toward an increase of population, and a profound economic unbalance. Though the consequences that flow from these two sources are not remarkable at any given time or in any one area, their interactions are capable in the long run of extensively modifying the existing patterns of Mediterranean life. The most astute policy for maintaining stability in the Mediterranean is subject to slow frustration if it overlooks their broad operation.

The Mediterranean region is peculiarly susceptible to their influences. The social consequences of an increase in population are rapidly felt in a region whose capacity to absorb additional manpower is strictly limited. Agricultural yields are already low throughout the region when measured in terms of the number of persons engaged in their production. Since no adequate alternative means have yet been developed for productively using additional labor, a growing labor force can result in nothing but further pressure on already limited resources. Alternative uses of labor cannot be quickly organized without external assistance.

The region as a whole is economically backward in the sense that industrialization has not reached the point where additions to the labor force are readily absorbed. The application of private foreign capital to this purpose has been haphazard. Industrialization by public capital, though frequently planned, has not been effectively got under way.

The rationalization of agriculture does not by itself solve the social problem of an expanding population. The methods so successfully employed during the war by the technicians of the Middle East Supply Center to increase production merely prove what can be done under special conditions and without cost accounting.

The total situation is such that, unless broadly planned and carefully applied external aid is introduced, progressive maladjustment can be anticipated.* The operation of these related demographic and economic factors has such a direct bearing on the long-run usefulness of the American position in the Mediterranean that a fuller examination of them is justified.

THE DEMOGRAPHIC TREND [1]

It is customary to note four stages in the recent demographic history of Europe: (1) a rapid decline in the death rate, followed by (2) a consequent large expansion of population; (3) an accelerating decline in the birth rate, followed by (4) a stabilization or even a decline in population. The Mediterranean region and southeastern Europe are now passing through the second of these stages, while Western Europe generally is reaching the end of the third stage. Projections of population to 1970 find the Mediterranean region still in the second stage and Western Europe in the fourth. Demographically, therefore, the southeastern and southern regions of Europe, the Middle East, and North

---

* The introduction of private capital at particular points and for particular purposes can no longer be considered a sufficient solution. At most, it creates limited sectors of artificial improvement without affecting the basic situation. The influx of private American capital into Saudi Arabia may, in fact, complicate the basic situation by providing excessive and irrelevant stimuli in too limited an area.

Africa are expanding relatively to Western Europe. The probable effects of this trend on the social structure of the Mediterranean region are likely to be profound.*

In terms of productive manpower—that is, the age group of 15 to 65—the net increase for Europe as a whole (west, east, and south) will be 20,000,000 between 1940 and 1970. But this net increase will be divided, $\frac{9}{10}$ for eastern and southern Europe, and $\frac{1}{10}$ for Western Europe. In the military age group—15 to 34—every country in Western Europe will have fewer men by 1970 than it had in 1940. Greece, Yugoslavia, and Rumania, on the contrary, will show a 20 per cent increase. †

The magnitude of this shift in manpower balance does not imply an inevitable shift in total power potential from the west to the east and south during the same period. Technological and other significant inequalities will modify, for a considerable time, the full effect of any alterations. Its significance lies rather in its capacity to affect the social and political stability of the regions concerned.

The chief areas of population growth in and around the Mediterranean are precisely those least prepared economically and socially to absorb increasing numbers. Not only are they underdeveloped industrially, but because of their low per capita agricultural production, they face an already heavy pressure on their land. For this reason demographic

* Present trends for Europe ". . . suggest sweeping, even dramatic, changes in the future, . . . show a slow process of population change too strong to permit the permanent maintenance of rigidly fixed economic and political arrangements." Notestein, *op. cit.*, p. 43.

† Comparable projections have not been made for the Arab states or for North Africa. The indicated trend, however, is in the same direction; and it is the direction that is significant at this point not the actual rate at which change is taking place.

For the figures given above *see* Notestein, *op. cit.*, pp. 119, 121.

change will presumably be translated with some speed into economic and social tensions, and these in turn will be expressed as sharp political issues. Political issues will tend to appear in the form of ideological conflicts or as diversions of tension by nationalistic attacks on external influences.

Before moving from these broad demographic forces to their economic correlates, other consequences of change in the population structure of contemporary societies must be noted. These factors indirectly and subtly condition relations between one culture and another by focusing aspirations and establishing common denominators of mass opinion. The most significant is the different old age and dependency structure of the West and of the East, with consequent differences in social attitudes and institutions.

The positive aging of the population of Western Europe—the United States can be included because the structure of its population corresponds more closely with that of Western Europe than with the region under consideration—shows itself in manifold ways. The most marked, however, is in the development of new institutions and in the modification of old ones in order to maintain and extend social security. A social structure is desired and deliberately sought which will be less fluid, less subject to sudden change, and which will work primarily to conserve benefits, standards, and values already achieved.

In this sense, the United States and Western Europe are, in their own judgments and in the appearance they present to the rest of the world, well-to-do regions concerned with the maintenance of a high standard of consumption and services. It is considered inevitable that peace and stability should mean to them first the protection and secondarily the extension of their gains. To other nations and peoples, however, stability and peace mean simply the opportunity to begin to try to achieve similar benefits.

Thus a profound psychological gulf develops. "The peoples of well-to-do areas want not only further opportunities for economic development but also the world security necessary to protect their gains. Those who live in undeveloped areas want an even greater economic development sufficient to overcome their poverty in comparison with other regions." *

The only really solid bridge across this gulf is a material one: consumer goods, heavy equipment, capital investment, and the extension of industrial and administrative techniques. It cannot be surprising that American and British Information Centers in economically backward regions find that an interest in technical journals and in techniques of organization and production is greater than the interest in democracy or in American and British history.

In the past many of Western Europe's gains overflowed into its eastern and southern fringes in the form of piecemeal industrialization, surplus goods, training in special skills, and improvements in public services and education. The postwar decline in these benefits serves merely to deepen the psychological gulf described above and leads to exacerbated doctrinal conflict and political instability. It does not matter whether such a decline is traceable to the momentary dislocations of the war or to deeper disturbances in the structure of populations. The immediate practical consequences are the same—tensions leading to instability.

---

* Moore, *op. cit.*, p. 25.
Standards of consumption in Western Europe, though showing a decline when measured against those of the United States and Western Europe's own past, still have a favorable margin over the standards in Eastern Europe and the Mediterranean region.

If the objective of policy is to maintain stability in the Mediterranean region, and if stability is in part dependent on the reduction of social and political tension within the states and social groups that make up the region, it matters greatly that the steadily operating causes of instability should be adequately understood. The need for this becomes more pressing when demographic change is seen in relation to the economic structure of the Mediterranean. At this point the problem becomes more than a mathematical projection across thirty years. It becomes one of immediate situations calling for immediate attention.

When President Roosevelt returned from Yalta, he remarked to Frances Perkins, "But, you know, the reason the East is so explosive is because people are so poor. They haven't enough to eat. They haven't enough possible occupations." It may be questionable to put poverty and political unrest in the relation of cause and effect, but it is not unreasonable to join the evidence of a demographic trend and the fact of economic backwardness and to see them as cumulatively interacting to break down an existing social structure.

THE ECONOMIC STATE OF THE MEDITERRANEAN REGION [2]

The basic economic fact in the Mediterranean is that the major part of its population is engaged in agriculture, even though the land provides productive work for rather less than three-fourths of the labor force thus employed. Even in areas where the per acre yields compare favorably with the more highly developed agriculture areas of the world, the per capita yields are invariably low. This regional characteristic becomes a source of social disequilibrium, not so much in itself as in consequence of the increasing pressure of population on the limited and undiversified resources of the region.*

An excess agricultural population has had two social and political consequences. It has fostered the preservation of antiquated forms of landownership and land use, and it has permitted the landowner to occupy a favored position between the peasant masses and external financial and political interests. The traditional social pattern of overlord and peasant accordingly permitted small groups of individuals to exercise a dominance which was perpetuated on the one hand by the pressing needs and the immobility of the unemployed agricultural masses and on the other hand by the natural preference of external interests for aligning themselves with the obvious holders of local power. In the Arab world, where this position was still further strengthened by tribal custom, local sheiks consistently acted as the channels through which outside influence operated. In the Balkans, and in southern Italy and Spain where industrialization was spotty, the local capitalist shared this function with the landowner, and the pattern of overlord and peasant was transferred with little alteration to the relations of owner-manager and worker.

The usual recommendations for changing the direction in which this sort of economic system drifts and for enabling it to check and then bring under control its own instabilities are not easily applicable to the Mediterranean region. These recommendations consist of reproducing, under control and

* In southeastern Europe the active farm population in 1940 was about thirty million, of which six to eight million could have been diverted to other labor without loss to agricultural production. The projected increase of 30 per cent in the labor force of this area in the present generation comes almost entirely in the farm population.
See Mandelbaum, *op. cit.*, p. 2.

at a higher rate of speed, the economic stages through which Western Europe passed in the course of the nineteenth and early twentieth centuries: (1) the rationalization of agriculture; (2) industrialization; (3) emigration. Under present conditions only the two first have any validity, and even their application requires such a degree of planning, authoritative control, and external assistance as to make it almost impossible to shift the problem from the level of theory to the level of effective action.

The outline of the problem and the conditions of its solution are clear and generally agreed upon, at least by specialists. Rapid industrialization is needed if the growing labor force is to be productively employed and if the pressure upon present production in all fields of economic activity is to be relieved. The basis of rapid industrialization is the provision of capital. To secure capital by gradual accumulation, as was done in Western Europe, is too slow a process where populations are increasing and where economic development has been so retarded. The only available sources are export capital from foreign powers or planned withholding from internal consumption.*

Even if the availability of capital from abroad could be assumed, its application would have to be controlled if it were to contribute effectively to the establishment of social

* All types of capital accumulation can be found in the Mediterranean region at the present time:

(a) foreign export capital in connection with the exploitation of petroleum fields in the Middle East and in connection with the development of Palestine as a Jewish state;

(b) grants-in-aid in Turkey, Greece, and Italy, accompanied by varying degrees of intervention;

(c) traditional investment capital in Spain, Italy, French North Africa, and Egypt;

(d) withholding from consumption in Yugoslavia and the Balkan satellite states, where the pattern is similar to that used by the Soviet Union;

(e) concentrations of domestic private capital by various devices of expropriation in the Soviet sphere of influence.

stability. Furthermore, its use for this purpose would have to be supported by new fiscal systems, extended public services, and sympathetic local authorities. This in turn implies the pre-existence of stable governments capable of giving continual effect to broad plans and of overcoming resistance to change on the part of groups whose interests are involved.

Finally, the character of the Mediterranean region does not offer much hope even to a regionally planned solution unless its economy can be made part of still more comprehensive plans. Its natural resources are poor. It is deficient in coal and water power. An intensifying world demand limits the use of its petroleum resources as an alternative source of power. Its minerals do not exist in important concentrations except for purposes of specialized export, nor are they usefully complementary as a basis for industrial development. Its surpluses of consumer goods are too similar to permit the organization of a significant system of internal exchanges.

A first-class dilemma is accordingly posed for the interested external powers. The Soviet Union is plainly not concerned to work toward an internal equilibrium for the Mediterranean as long as the region is an Anglo-American domain. Its immediate purpose must be to seek to multiply the sources of instability and to make it difficult to control existing ones. But in order to reap the maximum benefits from an unstable situation, the Soviet Union must make secure its position and influence in the Balkans.

This area, however, is as subject to the effects of overpopulation and underindustrialization as are the areas in the sphere of Anglo-American influence. Furthermore, the Communist governments of this area have committed the prestige of communism to the solution of these demographic-economic problems. Hence a plenitude of five-year plans, trade agreements, paper drafts for integrating local economic systems, and schemes to federate politically have appeared. But it is hard to find any evidence that genuine solutions have been found. The capital essential for an effective attack can only be accumulated under present conditions by withholding it from consumption. Foreign sources are choked off by political inhibitions among both communists and capitalists, the former fearing penetration and the latter fearing to give aid and comfort to a professed opponent.*

To create capital by deliberate withholding, even though the method is well understood and has been tested within the Soviet Union, raises as many problems as it solves when it is applied in areas where the margin of subsistence is already thin and the immediate result must be to intensify scarcities. Its application in circumstances where one cannot assume a rough loyalty to Communist principles and to a regime based upon them requires the establishment of the absolute controls of a police state. This is as likely to produce antagonism, political reaction, and resistance as it is to lead to a new economic order or to make a strategic position secure.

A complicated situation has resulted in which Soviet policy is concerned to create a new pattern of social stability in the Balkans while, in other parts of the Mediterranean, it works

* There is no doubt that an immense effort is being made to shape a Danubian federation and there is little doubt that the Soviet Union has inherited German plans for creating economic self-sufficiency in such a unit along with the German investments that were made for that purpose. Some of the plans to integrate productive facilities have become fact, but it is still possible to note that the general plan must run a stiff race against time.

to augment instability in the interest of expanding the influence of both Russia and communism. The contradictions that result are hard to conceal and are in part responsible for that propaganda which describes social tensions as an inevitable result of a struggle between the communist and capitalist systems. To seek to undermine at one point and to fail to find a genuine solution at another are both explicable by reference to an interfering and antagonistic "capitalist imperialism." *

The dilemma is somewhat differently presented to the United States and Great Britain. The rapid re-establishment of even a provisional stability in the Mediterranean is essential to the effective use of their position there. But since neither power is politically free to impose a solution by force, they must rely on persuasion. Every effort in this direction runs into difficulties. On the one hand, as in Greece, the strategic demands of the moment absorb all available resources and none are left over for persuasion. On the other, even a brief but actual contact with the region reveals deep sources of instability that will not respond to short-term treatment.

Thus, looking beyond the immediate moment and considering what is implied in the long-term maintenance of the Anglo-American strategic interest, it becomes clear that a series of provisional stabilities is not enough. The problem is to convert any given provisional stability into a process by which the whole social and political structure of the Medi-

---

* The same tendency to find a bogy-man can be seen in British and American statements about Greece and Italy, where an inability to arrive at effective solutions is attributed to the activity of a competing ideology. While there is no doubt that Communist activity impedes the effort to stabilize these countries, a full explanation must include a reference to those factors that have little to do with either communism or capitalism.

terranean world will move toward rather than away from the kind of equilibrium that will suit American and British requirements. At the moment policy appears to be caught in a vicious circle. It must conserve strategic advantages. To do so, it must accept whatever provisional solution of regional instability it can devise. These solutions are rejected by events with monotonous regularity and an increased effort to conserve the strategic position is called for. The process shows every sign of becoming increasingly costly as it becomes less rewarding.*

Secretary Marshall's forthright description of the course of American policy in Europe since the war, as developed "to meet a series of crises and therefore of a somewhat disjointed character," [3] is peculiarly applicable to the Mediterranean aspects of that policy. The European Recovery Program is an indication that policy has been partially redesigned to meet these crises in terms of their more persistent causes, but it is not yet clear what the application of this program will be to the Mediterranean region. There is no sign that the approach will be regional or that it will lead policy out of the vicious circle in which it now operates. Plainly, the interest of the United States in the Mediterranean, even though strictly confined to the maintenance of a strategic position, cannot be preserved by easy improvisation.

* An awareness of this danger was shown at the time the Truman Doctrine was debated in Congress. It was then suggested that, by reorganizing Greek economy and enabling it to generate its own stability, a "chain reaction" might be started which would favor the American interest on an ever-increasing scale. Although such a development was theoretically possible, it would have been prevented in the particular instance by inadequate resources, inadequate planning, contradictory estimates of the course to be followed, and by the speed with which military demands outweighed all other considerations.

XVI. Stability

EXCEPT in the unlikely possibility that the United States will conduct its relations with the Mediterranean region from a purely humanitarian point of view, the key aim of an American policy for the Mediterranean will be to maintain its internal stability in order to be free to use it as a strategic unit. The validity of this objective and the estimate of what is needed to achieve it will depend on the judgment that is made of the balance between forces tending to break down and forces tending to hold together the diverse parts of the region.

Two major items stand as assets on the side of the forces holding the region together: the actual existence of an Anglo-American structure of power, and a widespread demand for the kind of economic benefits that the United States and Great Britain are alone able to provide. These are valuable assets since their influence can be made felt at all points within the region.

Military power in the form of ships and planes, equipment, and professional advice still calls forth an understanding response in the Mediterranean provided it does not appear to be locally coercive. Economic power has a more direct influence. It makes immediate claims on the material interests of the masses, stands as a primary factor in the hopes and plans of individuals, and provides a leverage for securing compromises.

Though British military power is suspect because of memories of past interventions, American military power is not at the moment in the same difficulty. Though British economic power is weakening, the commercial consequences of its decline have not yet been directly felt by the Mediterranean masses. The penetration of American economic power, as far as individual experience of it goes, has been of such a kind that it is not easily distinguishable from the British power it replaces or supplements. The broad shift in this respect has made no perceptible difference at the mass level. Even at commercial and political levels where the shift was appreciated and where it led to efforts to gain advantages by trying to play British and American private interests against each other, it was soon concluded that in all matters affecting the strategic use of the Mediterranean the two powers would act in close concert.*

These two sources of influence—military and economic—work throughout the entire region and are accordingly applicable to the regional problems of strategic unity and internal stability. Together they create and maintain a psychological atmosphere that is favorable rather than otherwise. They are, in addition, supported by other sources of influence—humanitarian, educational, religious, and cultural. Such influences, though always difficult to measure, do work to soften and reduce the fears and antagonisms that power automatically gives rise to. Proper information services and technical and cultural exchanges should be expanded as rapidly as possible and co-ordinated in every suitable way

* The exception was Palestine. In this instance, however, the assumption of close concert between the United States and Great Britain was invalidated by policy statements made in Washington and not by actual events which took place on the spot.

with these established influences. Every type of modern publicity should be brought discreetly to bear.

Finally, among the assets must be noted the absence of a competitor whose claims are in any way accepted within the region. While the Mediterranean nations might well wish to be quit of British and American influence, this is not tantamount to an acceptance of the Soviet Union as a replacement. In spite of the fact that the Soviet Union is free of the political liabilities that plague Great Britain and has no record of commercial exploitation, Russia appears primarily as a disintegrating force. She offers no economic advantages in an acceptable form and, though capable of exploiting internal conflicts, cannot at present make good her claims as an alternative center of power and influence.

On the debit side of the ledger the items are diverse. Some are internal, others wholly external. Still others have their roots outside the Mediterranean but penetrate it and find there soil in which to sprout new shoots. Listed in the following order, the most important adverse forces are: the tendency of the region to fall back into its older form of a frontier between an Arab-Moslem and a European world; the expansion of the Soviet Union into the Balkans, which tends to split the European sector of the Mediterranean along the line of the Adriatic Sea, and communism, which provides the opposition groups of the region with alternative social and political objectives.

The interaction of these tendencies is very complex. They motivate the most contradictory movements and both confuse and make dynamic a wide range of purely local issues. Their interactions are responsible for a development that has been very marked in the case of Greece—the inevitability with which an internal conflict becomes involved in larger international issues and is correspondingly insoluble except as the international issues are themselves resolved.

It is impossible to say which of these forces is the most significant threat to the stability and unity which American and British policy requires. It is probably not necessary to reach a conclusion in this respect. Any or all work against the long-term usefulness of the Anglo-American position.

The most difficult to assess and certainly the hardest to meet is the ideological penetration of communism. It has the advantage of providing a doctrinaire answer to the individual discontents that accumulate as insecurity spreads. This is not to say that communism provides a solution to the problems created by demography and economic backwardness; it is to say that communism, like Arab nationalism in a smaller sphere, brings formulas and simple explanations whose evocative values cannot be lightly dismissed. Its methods and its results are observable in the Balkans; and, although its success is still confined to this sector of the Mediterranean hinterland, it constitutes a force to be reckoned with in Italy and Spain, where it gives at least a verbal form to unfocused tensions. There have always been cleavages between the life and the social traditions of rural and urban populations in the Mediterranean. The uneven distribution of the material benefits that flowed from the Western world widened rather than closed these gaps. Into these interstices communism seeks to move, aligning itself with already established nationalist tendencies and utilizing to the full the local value of slogans calling for freedom from capitalist and imperial overlords.*

* Compare Crossman's impression: "In Cairo I could study an old-fashioned class war of feudal landlords and capitalists against peasants and workers, which was obviously developing toward a violent revolutionary

In those cases where communism as a local political force coincides with particular strategic interests of the Soviet Union, an external drive against the stability and unity of the Mediterranean region develops. This has occurred on the Greek frontier, in the area around Trieste, and to a lesser degree in Iran. In many ways such open efforts to weaken the Anglo-American position are easier to meet than are the operations of less definable forces.

The major achievement of this type of pressure to date has been the reorientation of the Balkans north of Greece. Soviet influence has drawn the area away from its previous Mediterranean relations and turned it into a projection of Russia toward the Mediterranean. The most significant aspect of this change is that the strategic usefulness of the Mediterranean has been partially weakened by the conversion of the Adriatic Sea into a strategic boundary.

The immediate consequence of this alteration was to stiffen Anglo-American resistance to any further attempts to exploit the situation thus created—a reaction that has shown itself most plainly in the conduct of relations with Yugoslavia. The more remote effects cannot be fully estimated. The possibility of more comprehensive change is, however, implied. The use of the Mediterranean as a strategic unit now involves the problem of supporting a boundary that runs north and south from the Baltic to the Adriatic Sea and a boundary that runs east and west from Iran to the Adriatic Sea. Italy and Greece are the southern anchor of the one and the western anchor of the other line. The angle formed by the meeting of these two boundaries is an

situation. . . . Its objective is not merely the eviction of the British . . . but the destruction of the present social system. . . ." Crossman, *op. cit.*, pp. 106 and 107.

area in which Balkan communism and Soviet interest press
heavily, for even small gains at this point may lead to large
benefits.

The last broad force to be considered is an Arab-Moslem
movement compounded of secular nationalism and religious
patriotism. This ill-assorted and still unformed ideology
can be and has been described from contradictory points of
view. It is so nebulous, both in its composition and its purposes, that it can be quoted to support almost anything one
chooses to say of it. It is examined here entirely in terms
of its capacity to affect the strategic unity and the internal
stability of the Mediterranean region.

Ignoring the fact that the Arab states from the Middle
East to Morocco are not a homogeneous body of Arabian
Moslems and that their needs and interests are not identical,
the Arab League asserts the grand objective of a self-contained, self-supporting, self-directing regional bloc. This
group of states, bound together by a common faith and by
common social tradition, is to stand as a unit, facing the
Western world across the Mediterranean and resting on the
broad Moslem belt which stretches across its rear from the
Atlantic coast of Africa to India.

The process of reaching this goal involves the exclusion
of all Western military power—the British from the Middle
East and Egypt and the French from North and West
Africa—and the taking over of all essential economic power
from Western hands. Future relations are to be such as are
proper between equal sovereign powers.

The statement of this aim, aside from the possibility of
achieving it, has a double significance for British and American interests. On the one hand it represents a political ideal
with which compromises must plainly be made in the general

interest of Mediterranean stability. On the other hand it represents an objective which the nearer it is approached the more the character of the Mediterranean region as a strategic unit will be altered; for if fundamental differences between the Moslem, the Christian, and the Communist states of the region are insisted on, the Mediterranean Sea will tend to revert to marking a boundary for the Arab and European systems. Such a change would not necessarily endanger American security. Its significance in this respect would depend upon the nature of American relations with the Arab world. If such a trend became clearly indicated, however, it would make it essential for the United States to develop relations of so intimate a kind with this new center of power as to amount to an alliance.

It is easy to point out that Arab thinking is indifferent to those administrative and organizational techniques that appear to be inseparable from a genuine power system in the modern world and that Arab feeling is intolerant of those scientific and economic disciplines which make a modern state possible. But it is not relevant to do so. Nor is it relevant to note that Arab nationalism has many contradictory aspects and makes many plans that have no roots in Arab or Moslem feeling. It is a temptation to use such knowledge to resist the claims of the Arab League at small points, but it does not touch the basic problem. A deliberate attempt to turn the loosely joined components of this nationalistic movement against each other by playing on their known jealousies and self-interests, a conscious policy of divide and rule, would prove self-defeating. Its most probable consequences would be those which are most to be avoided—the establishment of a temporary common ground between Arab nationalism and communism, and the creation of a widespread Arab xenophobia which would make good relations impossible for the foreseeable future.*

The unfocused feeling which moves behind the Arab League can only be met by a general spirit of accommodation and compromise. The League is motivated in sufficient part by a strong sense of historical continuity and can press its aspirations on a broad front by appealing to the traditions of a far-flung religious community. From the American point of view, given the uncertainties that are involved, it is essential that policy be based on a few simple considerations. These are: the need to prevent a dangerous power-vacuum from forming in the Middle East, and the need to persuade the Arab world that its political unification has the co-operative and non-interfering interest and encouragement of the United States.

* In Palestine, for example, the strength of the Arab League is being subjected to a realistic test, and its inflated claims are being openly questioned. Yet even if the League does not live up to its pretensions, it will survive their exposure. The diplomatic efforts of Great Britain to avoid being involved in the exasperation that will certainly accompany this exposure is good evidence of the significance the Arab League is felt to have as a force in international relations even though its position as an effective power is doubtful. American policy has not yet hit on a satisfactory method of restraining exaggerated political claims without alienating a powerful political force.

XVII. The Basis of Policy

THE maintenance of strategic unity and the establishment of a new internal equilibrium are the linked objectives of American policy in the Mediterranean region. During and since the war improvisations to these ends were supported by definite resources of power and have had a limited success. These resources, though considerably reduced and weakened, are still available. Although improvisations will probably continue to be made until their inadequacy becomes self-evident, it must be hoped that, before this point is reached, circumstances will have begun to reveal the need for a coherent regional approach.

The existing means of enforcing a provisional stability and of retaining a rough-and-ready strategic unity have been mentioned in passing. They are the combined resources of an historical British system of authority and influence and an influx of American power based on a vast economic and military potential. These combined resources have been used in a variety of ways. Military power has been employed in the form of police activities in Palestine and in Greece by the British, and in Venezia Giulia by an Anglo-American occupation force. It has taken the form of conventional shows of naval force by the United States. It has been less directly applied in the form of equipment and technical advice in Greece and Turkey by the United States, and in Iraq and Trans-Jordan by Great Britain.

Economic power has been lavishly used in the form of

loans, gifts, grants-in-aid, and charity. The chief recipients have been Italy and Greece, but conventional subsidies and political loans, American as well as British, have been made to various Arab states.

Finally, indirect intervention in local affairs has also been employed in Italy and Greece and occasionally in the Middle East at times of crisis. Its value as a method is, however, limited by the resistances it creates. It tends to play into the hands of local opposition groups and adversely affects the long-term aim of building up friendly co-operative relations.

The effectiveness of these methods has clearly depended upon the position attained by Anglo-American authority during the war. And it must be emphasized that it has depended as much upon the existence and operation of a British system of influence as upon the resources of the United States. Neither, working alone, could have achieved equivalent results. An estimate of the present reality of this relationship is very pertinent to the discussion of American policy.

There is no doubt that the system of control by which Great Britain kept the Mediterranean geared to the service of British interests is weakening. In some respects the interests themselves have changed and parts of the system have become an expensive superfluity. In some ways the system is deeply marked by habits of overlordship which prevent its rapid adjustment to contemporary needs. The intangible quality of prestige on which it stood has been perceptibly lowered. But as a system it is still in place and must still be reckoned as a fact—an asset as seen by American policy, an obstruction in the Soviet view.

In the Middle East, where this system still retains elements of its imperial and semi-colonial origins, it has met with growing local antagonism. The visible forms of authority have consequently been increasingly laid aside in favor of a spirit of persuasion and of seeking accommodation with new political forces. In fact the system itself has undergone more profound changes than would be admitted by peoples who were habituated to resenting its mere existence. Theoretically the stage is set for a new order of British relations with the Middle East. In practice, however, the pace of change has been slower than the desires of local opinion. Egypt, possessed by a vigorous brand of nationalism and claiming the leadership of the Arab world, presses hard against the few restraints that the British system still maintains. In addition, Palestine has been used as a situation for testing the intentions as well as the strength of British authority.

Measured against immediate requirements, it does not seem as if the methods by which the British system has tried to modify and at the same time maintain itself have been wholly successful. Many observers, though it must be admitted that few of them have been entirely detached, have reported that events are outrunning the capacity of the system to control them. Yet, in spite of blocks in the negotiations with Egypt and in spite of an ambiguous balance between commitments and interests in Palestine, the British system still retains a considerable influence on their immediate course.* The system may be, as Walter Lippmann suggests, "unable to induce and certainly unable to impose solutions for the historic transition from empire to inde-

* The fact that the system has relaxed its control in Egypt and works there on the principle of "it is the considered policy of H. M. Government to consolidate their alliance with Egypt as one between two equal nations having interests in common" does not mean that the method of indirect control has been equally relaxed in other Arab states.

pendence"; but it is still in a position to slow down this transition by diplomatic rear-guard action. That this action has not taken the form of an attempt to divide in order to continue to rule is the best evidence possible of the completeness with which British policy is prepared to forego short-term advantages for estimated long-term benefits.

The significance of the British system of authority in supporting the American interest can scarcely be exaggerated. The effect in Greece of even a partial British withdrawal is a clue to what would follow if the Mediterranean region were suddenly free of this comprehensively penetrating influence. The competitive rush to fill the empty space would strain the present machinery of international relations beyond the breaking point, and would drive the Mediterranean states into a scramble of untested and unstable alliances.

The unvarnished fact of the moment is that the British system and American resources are a Siamese-twin power in the Mediterranean. The British system can no longer work effectively except in conjunction with American resources, and American policy cannot yet employ its resources effectively except in conjunction with the British system.

This system historically consisted of two parts: an organization of official and non-official administrators and advisers in the Middle East, and a less visible but no less important pattern of influence throughout the entire region. The whole was an organic growth made up of diplomatic experience, commercial exchanges, cultural contacts, long-standing and nearly always honored commitments, and strong strategic positions. In terms of trained personnel and accumulated local knowledge, it could not be easily or quickly reproduced.

An equivalent American system, devoted to maintaining Mediterranean affairs in a state suitable to support American interests, could not be put together by executive fiat or Congressional resolution. The creation of such a system is more than a matter of drawing up a table of organization. For the time being and in spite of obvious disadvantages, this Anglo-American relationship is inevitable, for no alternative authority is at hand.

There are practical difficulties in the connection from both the American and British points of view. Though we are concerned here mainly with the American side of the question, it is as well to understand that the British position has not been made easier by its need to rely increasingly on American resources. In peace time, when these resources are not available as part of an agreed military policy but come by Congressional appropriation for specific purposes, an uncertainty of no mean proportion enters into the operations of Anglo-American authority. Furthermore, policy-making functions in the American government are open to unexpected interventions from unanticipated quarters, and to be dependent upon the unpredictable is bound to be an uneasy experience.* But these are essentially difficulties of the short term.

The problem, from the American point of view, is a long-term one. The Mediterranean is in a state of flux. The ultimate pattern into which its component parts will fall is uncertain. It is assumed, however, on the basis of present American interests that relations between the United States and the Mediterranean region will continue to be important. Therefore the United States must guard its ultimate rela-

* The rapid shifts of ground on the part of the United States from 1945 to 1947 with respect to Palestine and the Arab states, the ambiguities introduced, and the false leads given in consequence are an example of the problem as seen by Great Britain.

tions by avoiding identification with the rancors and suspicions of the moment. Great Britain, by virtue of its historical past, now bears the brunt of regional ill will. It is of no conceivable value to the United States to find itself the receiver for this accumulated spleen.

The problem is to secure the required degree of correlation between the American and British interest without becoming committed in Mediterranean eyes to identical aims. Closely related is the problem of retaining freedom to act in the purely American interest without dangerously undermining the British system by which that interest is currently supported.

The full implications of the Anglo-American relationship in the Mediterranean have not been examined in a spirit of critical detachment or as a body of facts which set the limits of practical action. Such an analysis would show that at a large number of points American and British interests are identical. In so far as a joint position in the Mediterranean is being used to support interests which lie outside the region, agreement is as complete as need be for effective action. But when it comes to questions concerning the internal stability of the region, differences show. They arise in great part from the fact that the significance of the Mediterranean for the United States is by no means the same as for Great Britain.

As far as the internal affairs of the Mediterranean are concerned, there is scarcely any ground for comparing the interests of the two powers. It is possible to argue that the United States can be indifferent to the internal condition of the region as long as its strategic position is assured. The same cannot be said of Great Britain. British interests are highly diversified and involve the well-being of hundreds of thousands of individuals. They consist of a network of insurance services, shipping services, banking services, technical services, private investments, and export and import agencies. From long-established centers within the region, commercial, technical, and governmental agencies carry on co-ordinated activities which affect remote areas in Africa. Their operation, on no matter how reduced a scale, is an essential if unremarked feature of the daily lives of Britishers, Mediterranean peoples, and distant natives. A conventional responsibility for maintaining these activities still adheres to the British system of authority.

It is only reasonable that American policy should wish to avoid becoming involved in the support of such interests. But in order to do so without endangering a relationship that is so evidently necessary, American policy must develop a thorough understanding of the social and political character of the Mediterranean. On this foundation a completely independent American approach becomes ultimately possible. Short of this, however, a working compromise must be made between the disadvantages of and the necessity for this mutual dependence of American power and British influence.

XVIII. The Form and Limits of Policy

AT the moment the war in Europe ended, there were pre- sumably four courses open to the United States with respect to the Mediterranean:

(1) To withdraw entirely.
(2) To underwrite the British position.
(3) To maintain a combined Anglo-American position.
(4) To establish and provide for an American position.

In practice, however, there were only two courses. Events had already eliminated the possibility of withdrawing, and the state of domestic opinion put the establishment of a purely American position beyond serious consideration.* The remaining alternatives were so closely related that it was not necessary to choose between them. In fact both were followed. American policy worked through a combined Anglo-American position and by so doing, tacitly under- wrote the British position.

In a sense this was inevitable. The Anglo-American posi- tion was a solid fact in 1945. Allied Force Headquarters was a well-knit and functioning machine. The Middle East

* The historical section of this study shows that tripartite relations had developed sharp corners before the German surrender and that the sharpest of these corners was in the Mediterranean region. Even if withdrawal was considered early in 1945, the notion was abandoned by June of that year. At the time the speedy and confused redeployment of American force was incorrectly interpreted as indicating a policy of withdrawal. Actually it indicated no more than that policy was bending to the political pressure exerted by domestic opinion.

Supply Center was in full operation. American and British diplomatic agencies, though officially acting unilaterally, maintained close relations in the Mediterranean and looked to the remaining combined agencies for support.

The only genuinely debatable issue since 1945 has been: what use is to be made of the Mediterranean position and how is it to be maintained? The possibilities varied. The alternatives were never exclusive and official judgment never reached a clear decision. The information is not available for giving an account of the discussions that must have taken place, but the various points of view that entered into them can be guessed at. One was a minimum view which saw the possibilities in terms of a basically military definition of national security. Its chief concern was to keep the region from being dominated by the Soviet Union. It thought of the Mediterranean and developed its proposals in terms of defensive positions, lines of communication, and the maintenance of order.

The other was a maximum view. While not denying the validity of the purely defensive estimate, it saw more possibilities in the Mediterranean than standing pat. As a judgment it was never very clearly articulated or precisely defined, but it derived from a desire both to make safe and to extend that comprehensive set of values known as "the American way of life" and was supported by the opinion of humanitarian, internationalist, and commercial groups, as well as by those uncritical assertions about democracy that have always had a share in the formation of American opinion. The popular version of this view held that the Mediterranean should be helped to achieve democratic values, following which the Mediterranean states would form one of the centers from which Western concepts of law, order, and human worth could expand.

The official form of this opinion laid less emphasis on the conversion of the Mediterranean world to democracy. It agreed that freedom was desirable and important, but believed that freedom meant freedom for Mediterranean states to develop according to their own values. The United States primarily wanted them to be strong and healthy structures, free from external interference, and able to participate effectively in international life. American security required, however, that such a policy be accompanied by the means to prevent the Soviet Union from interfering, directly or indirectly, with this political growth.

In general, the limited and defensive point of view took precedence. Its case was supported by the fact that the Mediterranean soon became only one among many claims on national attention and, except when it was a scene of crisis—as in Greece in 1947 or Palestine in 1948—tended to fall into a subordinate place. Its claims for allocations of attention and resources were closely examined and grants of both were made on a restricted scale. Actually, the dividing line between a policy of using the Mediterranean position defensively and a policy of using the Mediterranean dynamically was not a sharp one. Problems were not presented in a form which forced a final choice; in fact they usually permitted both points of view to work simultaneously.

But this entire question had an important implication from the very start. Any policy that used the Mediterranean would sooner or later have to envisage a supplementary policy designed to ensure the stability of the region. A failure to appreciate this necessary consequence of having and using a position of power in the Mediterranean is the most obvious weakness of American relations with the region. The quickness with which opinion grasped the need to make strategic use of the region did not lead to an awareness of the concurrent need to put American relations with the region on a different footing.

The immediate uses to which the Mediterranean position is being put by the United States seem to be three in number. Momentary variations and the shading of one into the others can be ignored. The United States and Great Britain agree that the region shall not become a vacuum into which Soviet power can flow to the detriment of their global positions. Differences in their global interests are not an issue since it is assumed that both powers will be adversely affected by a change in this respect. Secondly, the United States and Great Britain agree on the practical necessity for resisting Soviet efforts to expand into the eastern Mediterranean and the Middle East. This includes blocking the Soviet Union from direct participation in Mediterranean affairs generally and refusing to admit the existence of a Soviet interest except of the conventional diplomatic kind. In the related matter of resisting Communist influence, their understanding is less firm. The British view does not entirely go along with the more rigid American attitude.

Finally, the Mediterranean position is useful in relation to plans to rehabilitate Western Europe. It represents an actual projection of American power. As such it provides the only readily available counterbalance to the military power which Soviet Russia has projected into Europe. In this sense it supplements by indirect influence the strength of those political forces in the various states of Western Europe that are willing to co-operate in a program developed under

American auspices. The position thus becomes a partial insurance against Soviet-Communist reaction to the European Recovery Program.

The essential thing about these uses is that they will and should exercise a definite influence over any policy designed purely to handle the internal affairs of the Mediterranean. It cannot be too bluntly asserted that the validity of a policy developed for the Mediterranean is contingent upon purposes that have little to do with the Mediterranean itself.

Thus limited, a policy for the Mediterranean must essentially be a regional policy and not merely the sum of diversified relations with the Mediterranean states, for its major objective will be to ensure the stability of a region. By this standard, any tendency to isolate and emphasize local problems is misleading. While there are daily Greek, Spanish, and Palestinian questions that must be handled locally and in local terms, these questions do not necessarily build up into a Greek, a Spanish, or a Palestinian problem. From the point of view of a regionally designed policy there are no such problems; there are instead Greek, Spanish, or Palestinian aspects of Mediterranean problems.

Unfortunately, tradition as well as the present organization of the Department of State encourages precisely this habit of diversification. Economic or strategic considerations may occasionally force a bird's-eye view, or a crisis may bring about temporary measures to concert information and instructions; but generally the routine conduct of business proceeds not on a regional basis, but through a multiplicity of channels.*

* Mediterranean information now comes into the Department of State by way of the Division of Middle Eastern and Indian Affairs, the Division of Near Eastern Affairs, the Division of Western European Affairs, the

The general principle of a regional approach is strongly re-enforced by particular elements in the situation. If the national interest is to be effectively served, three conditions must be satisfied in the Mediterranean. Its strategic value must be preserved. The essential interests of Great Britain and the United States must be co-ordinated to the utmost possible extent. The factors that produce internal tension must be checked when they cannot be eliminated.

The strategic value of the Mediterranean is in the long run as much impaired by a civil war in Spain as by a Soviet-inspired revolution in Iran. A steadily growing pressure of population in Greece contributes as much to the general instability of the region as does the same trend in Algeria. The economic backwardness of Greece presents the same general problem as the economic backwardness of Iraq. And finally, a failure to correlate American and British policy in Palestine creates the same difficulty as would a similar failure in Italy. Such things indicate the value of an approach whose main lines are set in terms of the region.

Barring the heightening of international tensions to the point of war—and it is assumed that it is still an objective in the policies of all the great powers to avoid this conclusion—it is possible that a limited use of the Mediterranean position as a defense against Soviet-Communist expansion might be all that American security required in the near future. If this is a valid judgment, the need for a supporting policy for the

Division of Southern European Affairs, the Office of Intelligence Research, the Office of International Trade Policy, and the Office of Information and Educational Exchange. There are certainly other and less easily identifiable channels in other government bureaus. Routine action flows out through the same channels.

See Department of State *Bulletin*, September 21, 1947, Vol. XVII, No. 429, p. 598 insert.

Mediterranean will not seem pressing. A minimum diversified policy of shoring-up the *status quo* would presumably
be enough to maintain the strategic usefulness of the region
over the next five- and perhaps even the next ten-year period.
The Anglo-American position is still favorable. The British
system of authority is still in place. Obvious points of tension
can be held in a prolonged, if irritating, stalemate as long
as a decision to go to war is not made. The cost of maintaining the position and of supporting the *status quo* through this
period will rise, however, if the cases of Greece and Italy
can be taken as examples. Mounting allocations of resources
will be called for to preserve the relative strength of the
defensive position, and the price of buying off intensifications
of social and political disorder will go up.

But the real difficulty is that a minimum policy does not
take into account what the Mediterranean region will be like
at the end of this short-term period. During the next five or
ten years demographic, economic, and ideological forces will
be working against any subsidized or imposed stability. The
full impact of such forces may not be felt within this period,
but that they will have to be reckoned with in any longer
term is becoming more and more certain. If a Mediterranean
policy of the United States sets its sights too low, the probable
effect will be artificially to check social and political rear-
rangements in the region. Under these conditions policy
ends up with a situation which, if not actually explosive,
can scarcely be described as serviceable to the American
interest.

Unless it can be assumed that there will be fundamental
changes in the relations or in the relative positions of the
great powers and that the Mediterranean will cease to be a

factor in American security,* reliance on what will work for
the short term and indifference to what may be needed for
the long term is a dangerously narrow approach. There are
grounds for thinking that the Mediterranean will long remain important to American security. The geographical
position of the region suggests that a Mediterranean policy
must look beyond the bare minimum even in the short term.
Though the region will continue to be essentially a means to
an end as far as the United States is concerned, policy cannot
begin too soon to study what is needed beyond force to
maintain the American position there.

The general design of a regional policy can be sketched as
follows. It would be a subordinate policy since its main point
of reference would be set by the place of the Mediterranean
in the larger pattern of American international relations. Its
objective, broadly stated, would be to fit the Mediterranean
into this place. Such a purpose is not as unmitigatedly self-
centered as it seems to be when put down in words, for in
order to achieve such an end, the well-being of the Mediterranean states must be given full consideration. The relations developed by such a purpose would probably be as free
from coercion as is possible in relations between strong and
weak nations.

Within this frame of reference a regional policy would

* The kind of changes meant would be:
   (a) a clear shift in the main lines of global strategy which would leave
the Mediterranean a global backwater;
   (b) an effectively functioning international security organization which
could reliably maintain the Mediterranean as an "in-between" region of
small independent states;
   (c) a decision frankly to subsidize Great Britain as the sole great power
in the region;
   (d) the political development of the Mediterranean states to the point
where they would of themselves constitute a center of power and act as
such in a global balance.

follow two lines. One would be concerned with the factors that operate regionally—population changes, economic maladjustments, ideological loyalties, the application and effect of scientific techniques. The other would be concerned with individual states and areas—their particular interests, internal tensions, political stabilities. These two lines would develop hand in hand, the one marking out the general problems and suggesting broad long-term patterns of action, the other accumulating relevant intelligence, handling local issues, and converting the general pattern of action into forms suitable for application in varying local circumstances.

More specifically, a regional policy would be concerned to prepare the Mediterranean region to absorb the accumulating effects of demographic change, to develop such economic potential as it possesses on a regional rather than on a competitively national basis, and to encourage rather than to resist the growth of political structures that have genuinely indigenous roots. In addition, it would seek out and strengthen those local political elements that are judged most able, not necessarily to maintain the *status quo,* but to provide the basis for a more stable regional equilibrium.

To be concerned with such matters implies a more thorough-going commitment in the Mediterranean region than American opinion is ready to accept. Yet the general principle has been laid down clearly enough in basic policy statements. The most recent is that of Secretary Marshall:

> [This country] must finish the task of assisting these countries to adjust themselves to the changed demands of a new age, or it must reconcile itself to seeing them move in directions which are consistent neither with their own traditions nor with those of this country.

In the latter case, the United States would be faced with a radical alteration of its own position in the world.[1]

The application of this principle to the Mediterranean region would involve a different method than does its application in Western Europe. It would require, for one thing, a more conscious and deliberate degree of intervention in its early stages in order to ensure that the impetus given would actually set the region moving in the desired direction.

Regional solidarity has been an even less conspicuous feature of Mediterranean than of European history. External pressures have encouraged competition rather than the search for a common ground. National, racial, and religious consciousness has flourished, both by nature and as compensation for an obviously subordinate position in the contemporary scheme. Assistance if accompanied by intervention is certain to be exasperating and to give rise to charges of imperialism. While it cannot be an insurance against this response, a clearly regional policy, since it would not be developed with specific reference to any one state but in terms of the relations of all within the region, should have a more softening effect than any other line that might be taken.

Certainly an attempt to deal with such matters by means of diversified diplomatic contacts cannot be expected to produce equally satisfactory results. The need to maintain these local contacts is not denied. The importance of a direct and freely responsible handling of nearly all kinds of daily problems is as great as ever. But the sum of these activities does not add up to a policy for the Mediterranean. From the point of view of the United States, the whole of the Mediterranean region is greater than the sum of its parts. If Greece comes under Communist control, the whole Mediterranean will be affected, or if Arab feeling is exacerbated, the consequences will be widely felt. These are statements of more than strategic formulas. They include the idea of broad forces —social tensions, political antagonism, competing ideologies —being released to work with accumulating vigor over a large area.

There is little doubt that a noticeable change has taken place in the general character of the pressures upon the Mediterranean region. They are fewer in number, but their intensity has been stepped up, their effects are more widespread and uniform. Furthermore, they work without much reference to national boundaries or to the national integrity of local states. A regional policy is able to adapt itself to this new condition and can work on a scale comparable to that of the problems it must handle.

The idea of a regional policy has been stated as if there were a sharp distinction to be made between it and the existing method of working through diversified contacts. This is not in fact the case. The difference lies rather in habits of mind than in daily procedures. A regional approach demands little more at the start than a widening of the field of vision. After that, practice and experience gradually bring the existing machinery of diplomatic decision and action into conformity with the new point of view.*

* An additional advantage of the regional approach can be mentioned in passing. It offers a better basis for protecting the national interest against domestic pressures which urge the adoption of particular courses of action. Domestic group interests, especially if they exert political influence, are always difficult to resist in the American system of government, and their operation can affect the national interest in unconsidered and irrelevant ways. Within the range of this study such influences have conspicuously intervened on three occasions to divert policy from its course—in Spain, in Italy, and in Palestine. Diversified policies, simply because their frame of reference is harder to state, are less able to resist such pressure than a regional policy would be.

The United States became a Mediterranean power at a moment of peculiar instability in the region's history. External and internal forces contributed to make it so, and definite social trends will apparently work to keep it so. The conventional formulas by which Mediterranean affairs were previously described have lost much of their validity and their continued use introduces a dangerous unreality into discussions of policy. Only a dogmatically enthusiastic mind would dare assert what the combination of forces acting upon and within the region will be in five, ten, or twenty years. Certainly no responsible maker of policy will feel the happiness of having made a sure judgment for some time to come.

The view that the United States takes of the Mediterranean is bound to remain a double one. On the one hand it will see the region as a factor in its relations with the Continent, as a factor in its relations with the Soviet Union, and as an item in its calculation of its position as a world power. On the other hand it will be increasingly obliged to consider the region as an organic fact, a complex and living structure whose parts are conditioned by widely different pasts and wildly divergent aspirations and which, as a whole, is disturbed by long-term trends. No matter how generally it is agreed that these two attitudes are complementary, a severely logical co-ordination of the policies they give rise to is out of the question. Failures to adjust them to each other will probably continue to plague relations with the region as well as to weaken the American position within the region. If the difficulty is to be solved at all, it is more likely to be solved by a series of almost unconscious adjustments to experience than by executive decision or Congressional action.

A regional approach, gradually building up into a regional policy, though it will not provide final answers, does offer a better chance to profit more quickly from experience. Without it there is a real danger of ending up with an elaborate but unserviceable structure of dispersed local commitments, the result of attention shifting from a pressing need to support a strategic position to a pressing need to deal with a localized issue. Such a construction could easily assume the character of a vital interest and its claims would be hard to dismiss, for every element in it would soon seem vital—as every block in a child's house is important because the displacement of one collapses the whole. The present state of the Mediterranean, taking into account the part that the region now plays in the pattern of American security and considering its own internal tensions, calls for more adequate treatment. It calls for a policy that is pliable in local detail and firm in its regional intent.

XIX. The Global Scale

THIS study cannot be brought to an end without looking at the question: What, after all, is the real significance of the Mediterranean for the United States? Admittedly the immediate importance of the region rests upon the fact that events have marked it out as an obvious place in which to attempt to check direct and indirect Russian expansion. But this may be a passing phenomenon. The answer really depends upon an estimate of the place of the Mediterranean region in the contemporary world and upon the judgment that American policy makes of the kind of world system in which the United States may find itself in the near future. This, in turn, is related to the kind of world system the United States desires and tries to build up.

The alternative possibilities can be summarized as follows. The United States can decide that it will probably be one of two powers in a Two-Power system. Since such a system cannot easily be imagined as coming to a point of balance, it must be assumed that it will tend to move irresistibly toward a One-Power system by way of war. The United States can try to avoid this eventuality by working to revive other powers and thus re-establish a Balanced-Power system on a global scale. The United States might seek to develop the United Nations organization to the point where it could act as a world government and establish what might be called a constitutional One-Power system. Or the United Nations, since it preserves the memory of a world in which many powers took part in the maintenance of a balance of power and since its very existence presupposes that such a world is more than a fiction, might act in parallel with American policy to avoid the establishment of a Two-Power system as an incontrovertible fact. Finally, the United States can prepare for the worst—a Two-Power world—and yet simultaneously try to create a Balanced-Power system by encouraging and contributing to the revival and maintenance of independence in small countries throughout the world.

While it is not possible to say with certainty that any one of these choices momentarily guides basic American policy, the signs point to an unwilling acceptance of the probability of a Two-Power system coupled with the intention of trying to revive some form of a Balanced-Power system. The extent to which the United Nations can support or must be considered as a stumbling block to these purposes is plainly not certain. But it can neither be wholly ruled out nor wholly relied on. The real significance of the Mediterranean can therefore be reasonably measured in terms of the place it would occupy in either a Two-Power or a Balanced-Power world.

The concept of a world in which only two centers of power—the United States and the Soviet Union—exist leads to two proposals. One envisages an immediate test of strength and proposes suitable action. The other anticipates an inevitable though deferred conflict and proposes suitable preparation. The Mediterranean appears as a key region in both cases. In relation to an immediate conflict it represents a strategic position whose features have already been described. Its place in relation to a conflict in the undetermined future is still more important.

It has been often remarked that the United States is automatically drawn into any war in which a single power threatens to emerge as dominant over the continent of Europe. Various explanations have been given for this fact, but none is so satisfactorily comprehensive as that which says that the United States cannot accept the organization of Europe's material, industrial, and manpower resources by a single power, since this would result in the formation of the one unit capable of outweighing American potential. This consideration would, by itself, explain the resistance of American policy to the idea of a Communist-dominated Europe.

But the problem also occurs in an expanded form. Two foreign wars fought on a global scale with modern technical equipment have made the United States conscious of its geographical position as an island lying between the European and Asiatic shores of the continental land mass of Eurasia. By a very reasonable extension of ideas, policy moves on to consider the consequences of Eurasia, rather than Europe, being under the domination of a single power. The rise of Russia as a modern state has introduced a practical note into this abstract speculation.

Suppose the Soviet Union were able to organize and command the material, industrial, agricultural, and manpower resources of Europe and Asia! The German menace seems feeble in comparison. Yet such a possibility has to be taken into account as soon as the idea of a Two-Power world forces itself on American attention.

If the position of the United States, in the year 1948, is examined in this light, courses of action rather quickly suggest themselves. The actual coastal areas of Eurasia are not under the domination of a single power though their present independence is precarious. Western Europe, China, India, and the Mediterranean region make up a belt of states that keep the Soviet Union away from the open seas and resist the idea of an organization of Eurasia by Soviet-Communist power. The Western European sector of this rim contains the largest concentration of industrial potential and skills outside the United States. The Mediterranean sector contains what is believed to be the largest proved oil reserve outside the Western Hemisphere. Furthermore, the Middle East area of the Mediterranean is the single land route by which a Eurasian power can move out of its area of authority.

It is not necessary to assume that the Soviet Union deliberately envisages an expansion ranging as far into the future as these observations might suggest. The natural tendency of a dynamic people to move wherever it finds no resistance would be all that was needed to convert opportunity into an implacably logical progression. The Mediterranean region offers a great opportunity in this connection in the sense that even a limited success there would bring about changes that would speedily build up into a cumulative process. Western Europe offers an almost equally fertile field, but there, success means control of industrial potential, while in the Mediterranean region it means the gain of a tremendous strategic advantage.

Since this situation is defined by geography and confirmed by the present distribution of raw materials, food-producing areas, industrial plant, and manpower, the real significance of the Mediterranean region lies in the fact that its control is very closely related to the problem of survival in a Two-Power world. Whatever the United States had felt obliged to do to prevent the domination of Europe by a single power, it would find itself obliged to do on a vastly bigger scale to prevent the domination of Eurasia by a single power. And if this could not be prevented, policy would then have to fix its attention on keeping the dominant power from breaking out.

This global picture strongly suggests that the Mediterranean will continue for the indefinite future to occupy an important place in the design for American security. Though the present interest in the Mediterranean can be adequately explained by reference to history and immediate necessity, there is little reason to doubt that it will imperceptibly expand as it takes the larger pattern of possibility into account.*

However, American policy must not be thought of as waiting supinely for so undesirable a probability to become a certainty. Actually policy will explore the means of guiding relations and, if possible, events into channels that do not inevitably lead to this end. The most obvious short-term step is to strengthen those countries which make up the coastal fringe of Eurasia. This process was begun with subsidies in Greece, Italy, and France. It grew into explicit support of Greece and Turkey in the Truman Doctrine. It is coming to full stature in the European Recovery Program. Its further development in the Mediterranean and its ultimate extension into the Far East should be no occasion for surprise.

Strength through subsidies has never been an acceptable method of international insurance and it is particularly unacceptable to American opinion. A more satisfactory method, in the American view, would be one which re-created a

---

* Reference to the atomic bomb and to other new weapons does not dispose of the considerations stated here. These weapons affect the problem of superiority in a Two-Power system but they do not alter the basic geographical relations of the powers concerned. Nor do they directly affect the possibility of organizing potential under a single authority.

genuine balance of power in the world.* This would mean that countries that are now being subsidized would have to be converted into real centers of power. The smallness of the unit would not greatly matter provided it was independent and internally stable and could not be coerced by one strong power without driving it into the arms of a competing strong power.

It would be the total weight of small independent centers of power that would constitute the third, the "in-between" element needed if power—now abnormally fluid in the world—were to be brought again into a balanced system. The American interest in checking the drift toward an unstable and dangerous Two-Power world does not require that the "in-between" units be satellites of the United States as the countries of Eastern Europe are satellites of the Soviet Union. It requires no more than that they be free and able to resist indirect domination. They need not, and in fact cannot, be made strong enough to resist domination by force unless they group themselves into coherent blocs of power. This objective need not be strained after. Armed aggression would in any event throw the international situation into its two-power form and the issue would be met on that basis.

The Mediterranean is plainly an important region for the development of a policy with these objectives. The difficulty of making it work is, however, great. The Mediterranean nations, with the exception of Italy, Spain, and Turkey, have not been independent powers within the term of modern history. Their ability to achieve and maintain independence is weak.

* Balance of power should not be understood as a flat alternative, and hence in opposition to a system of international organization. It should rather be taken to mean an equilibrium which, because it tends to prevent the movement of a two-power structure toward one-power hegemony, is a probable pre-condition of any successful international organization.

Their desire to reach this status is strong. A policy that sought to create a group of firm states in these circumstances would be forced to provide much of the straw to make its hoped-for bricks. But, except for this consideration, the policy is generally suited to the Mediterranean region. It would give admirable political support to the strategic position now being maintained there, for it would reduce the suspicion of intervention and dominance that accompanies the presence of power. Its clear application would give local reality to the position the United States has taken in the region and provide a consistent and easily understood explanation of American actions. The strategic purposes of the United States do not of themselves automatically enlist the diffused loyalties of Mediterranean peoples, but if those purposes were related to a process of building up centers of national strength, co-operation would be more readily found. Thus it is a valid line and in principle leads to a more reasonable conclusion than does a policy which assumes with finality a Two-Power world and bluntly acts on that assumption.

There are grounds for asserting that the Mediterranean region will persist as an important item in American foreign policy. Until a new pattern in international relations is clearly revealed and the United States is able to say with certainty that it is one pole of a Two-Power system, or that it is a major power coexisting with others in a Balanced-Power system, relations with the region will not come up for final re-examination. Instead, commitments will continue to be called for and will probably be required on a mounting scale. The diversified and ardent societies that form the Mediterranean—disordered by the accumulating effects of strong social trends, unanchored among competing loyalties, cohering uncertainly in response to dimly felt aspirations, and violently dissolving in consequence of unanalyzed fears —promise to be a long-standing and expensive problem in American foreign relations.

References

CHAPTER I

1. Speech to Foreign Policy Association, October 21, 1944, Department of State *Bulletin*, October 22, 1944, Vol. XI, No. 278, p. 448.

CHAPTER II

1. *Foreign Relations of the United States*, 1914, p. 906.
2. *Ibid.*, 1923, Vol. II, p. 916; 1930, Vol. III, p. 605; 1930, Vol. I, pp. 486-87.
3. *Ibid.*, 1929, Vol. III, p. 116.
4. *The American Naval Mission in the Adriatic, 1918-1921*, Administrative Service Reference Report No. 4, Navy Department, 1943, pp. 55-56.
5. *Foreign Relations of the United States*, 1923, Vol. II, pp. 884-86.

CHAPTER III

1. William L. Langer, *Our Vichy Gamble*, A. A. Knopf, 1947, p. 357.
2. Department of State *Bulletin*, Oct. 23, 1943, Vol. IX, No. 226, p. 271.
3. *Ibid.*, December 23, 1945, Vol. XIII, No. 339, p. 994.
4. See Hajo Holborn, *American Military Government*, Infantry Journal, 1947, Appendix, p. 133.
5. Department of State *Bulletin*, November 6, 1943, Vol. IX, No. 228, p. 308; June 24, 1944, Vol. X, No. 261, p. 573.

CHAPTER IV

1. Department of State *Bulletin*, October 1, 1944, Vol. XI, No. 275, p. 338.
2. *Ibid.*, October 15, 1944, Vol. XI, No. 277, p. 403.
3. *Ibid.*, August 6, 1944, Vol. X, No. 251, p. 336.

CHAPTER VI

1. *Parliamentary Debates* (Hansard), House of Commons, January 18, 1945, Vol. 407, No. 17, col. 398.
2. New York *Times*, April 11, 1947.
3. London *Times*, June 12, 1945.
4. Department of State *Bulletin*, December 17, 1944, Vol. XI, No. 286, p. 760.

CHAPTER VII

1. Department of State *Bulletin*, April 22, 1944, Vol. X, No. 252, p. 372; see also August 13, 1944, Vol. XI, No. 268, p. 153.
2. *Ibid.*, March 4, 1945, Vol. XII, No. 297, pp. 321, 324.
3. *Ibid.*, July 8, 1945, Vol. XIII, No. 315, pp. 50, 52.

CHAPTER VIII

1. The text was published in the New York *Times*, May 20, 1945.
2. Department of State *Bulletin*, May 13, 1945, Vol. XII, No. 307, p. 902.
3. *Ibid.*, June 3, 1945, Vol. XII, No. 310, p. 1013.
4. Private conversation in Athens, November, 1945.

CHAPTER IX

1. New York *Times*, August 16, 1946.
2. James F. Byrnes, *Speaking Frankly*, Harper, 1947, p. 155.
3. *Ibid.*, p. 153.
4. Speech to Overseas Press Club, New York *Times*, March 1, 1946.
5. Department of State *Bulletin*, October 20, 1946, Vol. XV, No. 381, p. 722.
6. *Ibid.*
7. *Chronology of International Events and Documents*, Royal Institute of International Affairs, September 23-October 6, 1946, Vol. II, xix, p. 592.

CHAPTER X

1. Richard Crossman, *Palestine Mission*, Harper, 1947, p. 199.
2. Full text in New York *Times*, March 13, 1947.

CHAPTER XI

1. New York *Times*, April 19, 1947; *The Economist*, July 5, 1947, p. 4.

CHAPTER XII

1. Speech to the Senate, June 4, 1932, quoted in Macartney and Cremona, *Italy's Foreign and Colonial Policy 1914-1937*, Oxford Univ. Press, 1938, p. 284.

CHAPTER XIII

1. Herbert Feis, *Seen from E. A.*, A. A. Knopf, 1947, pp. 115-121.
2. E. A. Speiser, *The United States and the Near East*, Harvard Univ. Press, 1947, p. 224.

CHAPTER XIV

1. Studies such as K. Mandelbaum, *The Industrialisation of Backward Areas*, Basil Blackwell, Oxford, 1945, and Wilbert E. Moore, *Economic Demography of Eastern and Southern Europe*, League of Nations, 1946, are useful in establishing the pattern and widespread operation of these tensions.

CHAPTER XV

1. Basic demographic studies for the region are: Frank W. Notestein, *The Future Population of Europe and the Soviet Union*, League of Nations, 1944; Wilbert E. Moore, *op. cit.*; Ernest Jurkat, "Prospects for Population Growth in the Near East," and Clyde V. Kiser, "The Demographic Position of Egypt," in *Demographic Studies of Selected Areas of Rapid Growth*, Milbank Memorial Fund, N. Y., 1944.
2. Basic studies are: K. Mandelbaum, *op. cit.*; P. E. P. (Political and Economic Planning) Group, *Economic Development in S. E. Europe*, Oxford Univ. Press, 1945; W. C. Lowdermilk, *Palestine, Land of Promise*, Harper, 1944.
3. Address to Governors' Conference at Salt Lake City, New York *Times*, July 15, 1947.

CHAPTER XVIII

1. Address to Governors' Conference, Salt Lake City, New York *Times*, July 15, 1947.

Index